D1466502

Date Loaned

THE FOOL

A PLAY IN FOUR ACTS

Photograph by White Studio

ACT III FROM THE SELWYN PRODUCTION

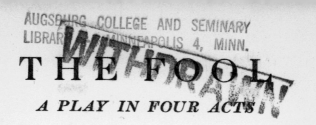

THE FOOL

A PLAY IN FOUR ACTS

BY

CHANNING POLLOCK

*"They called me in the public squares
The fool that wears a crown of thorns."*

PUBLISHERS

**BRENTANO'S : : : NEW YORK
BRENTANO'S LTD. : : LONDON**

PRINTED IN THE UNITED STATES OF AMERICA

The cast of "THE FOOL" as originally presented by
Selwyn & Company, at the TIMES SQUARE THEATRE,
New York, October 23, 1922

THE FOOL

PRODUCED BY FRANK REICHER

Scenic Production and Decorations by
CLIFFORD B. PEMBER

THE PERSONS
(In the order in which they speak)

Mrs. Henry Gilliam	MAUDE TRUAX
"Dilly" Gilliam	REA MARTIN
Mrs. Thornbury	EDITH SHAYNE
Mr. Barnaby	GEORGE WRIGHT
Mrs. Tice	LILLIAN KEMBLE
"Jerry" Goodkind	LOWELL SHERMAN
Rev. Everett Wadham	ARTHUR ELLIOT
Clare Jewett	PAMELA GAYTHORNE
George F. Goodkind	HENRY STEPHENSON
"Charlie" Benfield	ROBERT CUMMINGS
Daniel Gilchrist	JAMES KIRKWOOD
A Poor Man	FRANK SYLVESTER
A Servant	GEORGE LE SOIR
Max Stedtman	GEOFFREY STEIN
Joe Hennig	ROLLO LLOYD
Umanski	FREDRIK VOGEDING
"Grubby"	ARTHUR ELLIOTT
Mack	FRANK SYLVESTER
Mary Margaret	SARA SOTHERN
Pearl Hennig	ADRIENNE MORRISON
Miss Levinson	WANDA LAURENCE

And a Number of Persons of Minor Importance

The cast of "THE FOOL" as presented by Selwyn & Company, at the SELWYN THEATRE, Boston, Mass.

———

THE PERSONS

(In the order in which they speak)

Mrs. Henry Gilliam	MRS. STUART ROBSON
"Dilly" Gilliam	MARY MEAD
Mrs. Thornbury	HELEN HOLCOMB
Mr. Barnaby	GEO. W. WILLIAMS
Mrs. Tice	FRANCES BRANDT
"Jerry" Goodkind	A. J. HERBERT
Rev. Everett Wadham	CLARENCE HANDYSIDES
Clare Jewett	ALEXANDRA CARLISLE
George F. Goodkind	OSCAR FIGMAN
"Charlie" Benfield	FRANKLYN HANNA
Daniel Gilchrist	CHARLES MILLWARD
A Poor Man	BERTRAM MARBURG
A Servant	BRETTON KENNEDY
Max Stedtman	FRANK CONLON
Joe Hennig	HALE NORCROSS
Umanski	DAVID LEONARD
"Grubby"	CLARENCE HANDYSIDES
Mack	BERTRAM MARBURG
Mary Margaret	ZILLA INEZ SHANNON
Pearl Hennig	HILDA VAUGHN
Miss Levinson	VIRGINIA NORTON
A Girl of the Streets	EVE KOHL

THE PERSONS

(In the order in which they speak)

MRS. HENRY GILLIAM.

"DILLY" GILLIAM.

MRS. THORNBURY.

MR. BARNABY.

MRS. TICE.

"JERRY" GOODKIND.

REV. EVERETT WADHAM.

CLARE JEWETT.

GEORGE F. GOODKIND.

"CHARLIE" BENFIELD.

DANIEL GILCHRIST.

A POOR MAN.

A SERVANT.

MAX STEDTMAN.

JOE HENNIG.

UMANSKI.

GRUBBY.

MACK.

MARY MARGARET.

PEARL HENNIG.

AND A NUMBER OF PERSONS OF MINOR IMPORTANCE.

THE PLACES

Act I.—*The Church of the Nativity.*
            Christmas Eve, 1918.
Act II.—*The Goodkinds' Home.*
            November, 1919.
Act III.—*"Overcoat Hall."*
            October, 1920.
Act IV.—*Gilchrist's Room—"Upstairs."*
            Christmas Eve, 1920.

The action takes place in New York City.

INTRODUCTION

BY BASIL KING

It is safe to say that no one who sees *The Fool*, by Channing Pollock, will ever forget that he has seen it. That fact in itself will put this play into a list where it will have no more than a score or two of American plays as its companions. Apart from all questions of art, or taste, or opinion, or preference, is this test of vitality. The dynamic play endures in memory long after it has left the stage. It continues to be talked about; it helps to form a standard of comparison. When it comes back, as not infrequently it does, it impresses to some degree a second and a third generation as it impressed the year whose activities inspired it.

Energy and breadth are perhaps the qualities which *The Fool* reveals most strikingly. It is tense with life; its outlook is wide. Dealing with nothing trivial, or merely of to-day, it is vibrant with those passions and emotions of the hour which, all the same, are timeless.

Its theme is the biggest that can occupy the mind, the emergence of the human being out of the material into, or towards, the spiritual. Exactly what this means we have not the space to define, but, except for the most sodden, all of us can understand it. It is the business which, consciously or subconsciously, we are all about. Our methods may be diverse; our aim may often become deflected; but our objective is the same. To

11

struggle to something higher is the impulse of every human being ever born.

All the chief characters in Mr. Pollock's play are working that impulse out. The conflict springs from their understanding of what the higher consists in. Each follows his or her own Star of Bethlehem.

The point to be noted is that Gilchrist is the only one among the leading characters to take the course which every one else considers impractical, and yet the only one to work out a success. He is an illustration of that paradox, of which we are only beginning to understand the truth, that we must lose the world to find it. Ever since 1914 especially we have been confessing with our lips, and sometimes in our hearts, that the wisdom of man is foolishness with God. If we wanted a proof of it we should only have to lift our eyes and look at the topsy-turvy Europe, Asia, and America man's wisdom is creating. That wisdom is not only foolishness to God but is fast becoming mere foolishness to ourselves; and yet we see no remedy. The methods which we know in advance will not work, which have proved that they will not work a hundred thousand times in human experience, are the only methods we consider "practical." They have been the ways of "practical men" in government, business, diplomacy, religion, society, and war, ever since the beginning of time. We cannot bring ourselves to forsake them. We prefer to sink with the ills we know rather than run the risks we incur when trying to walk on the water.

THE FOOL

ACT I.

SCENE: *The Churcn of the Nativity. New York.*

The set, representing only the chancel, is as deep as possible, so that, even when its foreground is brightly illuminated, the detail back of that is lost in shadows. Pierced by three fine stained glass windows, the rear wall looms above the altar, on which the candles are not lighted. In front of that is the sanctuary, and, in front of that, the communion rail, with three steps to the stage. Just right of these steps is a very tall and beautiful Christmas tree. The tree has been expensively trimmed, and has a practical connection for an electric-lighted ornament still to be placed at its top. Down R., a door to the choir room, and, down L., a door to the parish house and the street. These doors are exactly alike. Down L., two folding wooden chairs that have been brought in for temporary use. A tall stepladder L. of the tree, facing front. Down R., two wooden boxes of ornaments, that on top open and half emptied. There is a pile of tissue-wrapped and ribboned packages under the tree, and a general litter of gifts, boxes, and crumpled paper everywhere. The Church of the Nativity is fashionable and luxurious;

13

*the effect of the set must be that of a peeping into a
building spacious, magnificent, and majestic.*

AT RISE: *Christmas Eve, 1918. The act begins in
bright day-light—about half past three in the afternoon—so that the early winter twilight may have set in
before its end. The sun's rays now come through a
stained-glass window above the door L., so that the R.
of the stage is bathed in white, the C. in blue, and the
L. in a deep straw. Two women and a girl are discovered.* MRS. HENRY GILLIAM, *bending over the box
down L., is fat, forty, rich and self-satisfied. Her
daughter,* DAFFODIL, *commonly called "Dilly,"
perched upon the ladder, is a "flapper." As regards
her mind, this means that, at twenty, she is wise and
witty, cynical and confident, worldly and material beyond her elders. Physically, she is pretty, and, of
course, has not hesitated to help out nature wherever
she has thought it advisable. Considering what has
been spent on her education, she is surprisingly ignorant and discourteous, particularly to her mother,
who bores her dreadfully.* LEILA THORNBURY *is a di-
vorcee; thirty, smart, good-looking, with something
feverish in her face, in her eyes, in her movements.
Deliberately attractive to men, she is disliked, in pro-
portion, by women. All three are very expensively
dressed. Mrs. Thornbury has laid aside a fur coat
on the cost of which twenty families might have lived a
year. She is at the end of the stage, concerned with a
number of dolls and other toys.*

Mrs. Gilliam

[*Turning with some ornament, on a level with her eyes she observes a generous view of* Dilly's *nether limbs*]: Dilly, for pity's sake, pull down your skirt! [*As* Dilly *pays no attention, she continues to* Mrs. Thornbury] I don't know what skirts are coming to!

Dilly

They're not coming to the ground, mother. You can be sure of *that!*

Mrs. Gilliam

What *I* can't understand is why our young women want to go around looking like chorus girls!

Mrs. Thornbury

Perhaps they've noticed the kind of men that marry chorus girls.

Dilly

Salesmanship, mother, begins with a willingness to show goods.

Mrs. Gilliam

Dilly! *Pull down your skirt!*

Dilly

I can't! That's all there is; there isn't any more!

Mrs. Thornbury

[*Holding up two dolls*]: What are we going to do with these?

MRS. GILLIAM

[*Despairingly surveying the profusion*]: Goodness knows!

MRS. THORNBURY

I've two engagements before dinner, and I've got to go home and undress for the opera.

DILLY

I gave up a dance for this.

MRS. GILLIAM

A dance at this hour?

DILLY

People dance at any hour, mother.

MRS. GILLIAM

What do they do it for?

DILLY

For something to do. [*To* MRS. THORNBURY] *We're* young and we've got to have life and gaiety; haven't we, Mrs. Thornbury?

MRS. THORNBURY

We've got to have something. I don't know what it is, but I know we have to keep going to get it.

MRS. GILLIAM

But you all waste your time so dreadfully. I'm busy, too, but my life is given to the service of others.

DILLY

What could be sweeter?

MRS. GILLIAM

Dilly! Nobody knows better than you that I've never had a selfish thought! Mr. Gilliam——

DILLY

Of the Gilliam Groceries, Inc.

MRS. GILLIAM

Mr. Gilliam says I'm far *too* good!

MRS. THORNBURY

We agree with him, Mrs. Gilliam.

MRS. GILLIAM

Only yesterday I gave five hundred pounds of coffee and sugar to the Salvation Army!

DILLY

And today father jumped the price of sugar to thirty-two cents!

MRS. THORNBURY

Now—Dilly!

MRS. GILLIAM

[*With rising emotion*]: One gets precious little reward. . . . I can tell you! I sent helpful thoughts from the Bible to all Mr. Gilliam's employes! Now they're on strike, and the man that got "Be content with your wages" is leading the strikers! . . . Where's the Star of Bethlehem? [*To conceal her agitation, she has turned to the box.*]

DILLY

It doesn't work, mother.

MRS. THORNBURY

Are those your husband's men—on the front steps?

MRS. GILLIAM

Oh, no! Those are people from the sweat shops! They're starving, I hear, and Mr. Gilliam says it serves 'em right! [*Bringing forth a small case*] What's the matter with the Star of Bethlehem?

DILLY

Oh, the usual! Whoever heard of the lights working on a Christmas Tree?

MRS. GILLIAM

[*Holding up the star*]: But this *must* work. Mrs. Tice had it made to order—of Parisian diamonds. It cost a hundred dollars.

DILLY

[*Reaching for the gewgaw*]: All right! It's better than nothing! [*She takes it, and starts to ascend*] Hold the ladder, mother! It wiggles! [MRS. GILLIAM *obeys.*]

MRS. THORNBURY

[*She has ribboned both dolls, and sets that just finished beside its companion on the chair*]: There! [*Rises*] I'm half dead, and there *can't* be any more presents! [*Starts up for her coat*] I'd give my left hand for a cigarette!

Mrs. Gilliam

Not here!

Mrs. Thornbury

I don't know why not. We've had almost everything else.

Dilly

Mother's so *Mid-Victorian!* And ministers are finding they've got to do *something* to make church-going attractive. What do we get out of it now? I've heard of preachers who go in for dances and movies, and they draw crowds, too. Naturally! Who wouldn't go to church to get a squint at Douglas Fairbanks? [*She has hung the star*] I'm through!

Mrs. Gilliam

Then come down.

Dilly

Believe me, I'm glad to get off this thing! [*She descends unsteadily*] When I think I broke an engagement with the best fox-trotter in New York to do a shimmy with a ladder——

[Mr. Barnaby, *package-laden, enters L. He is the sexton, and of the age, manner and appearance peculiar to sextons*] Oh, Mr. Barnaby!

Mrs. Thornbury

[*Turns and is appalled at his burden*]: What *have* you got?

Mr. Barnaby

Some more presents.

Mrs. Gilliam

Good Lord!

Mr. Barnaby

[*Deposits his bundles on the steps L.C.*]: Mrs. Tice brought them. She and Mr. Jerry Goodkind. [Mrs. Gilliam *nudges* Dilly] They're just coming in.

Mrs. Gilliam

[*Sotto voce*]: Dilly, powder your nose! [Dilly *takes her bag from the communion rail, and obeys*] Mr. Barnaby, our star won't light. Will you see if you can fix it? [Mr. Barnaby's *mind is on* Mrs. Tice. *She is much too rich to open a door. He is edging L.*]

Mrs. Thornbury

And Mr. Barnaby——[*Voices off L.*]

Mr. Barnaby

One moment!

[*He opens the door L. Enter* Mrs. Tice *followed by* Jerry Goodkind. Mrs. Tice *has just entered middle-age, and refuses to shut the door behind her. Her wealth, which has given her an air of great authority, has made it possible for her to look a smartly-dressed young matron. The truth is that she is clinging to youth in an ever-lessening hope of "keeping" her husband. Beneath the "air of authority" is something cowed, and worried, and unhappy. Just so, beneath the smiling, careless surface of* Jerry *lies iron. He can be*

*very ugly when he wishes, and he is always suffi-
ciently determined to get what he wants, though
he gets it generally by showing the urbane surface.
JERRY would describe himself as a "kidder." He is
35; sleek, well-groomed, and perfectly satisfied
with himself. His most engaging point is a per-
petual smile.*]

MRS. TICE

Hello, everybody! [*"Everybody" returns the greeting*] Who are those people on the church steps? A lot
of dirty foreigners blocking the sidewalk!

MR. BARNABY

It's the grating, Mrs. Tice. The furnace room's
underneath, and they're trying to keep warm.

MRS. TICE

Well, let 'em try somewhere else! [*Recollection of
unpleasant contact causes her to brush her coat*] I
don't mean to be unkind, but there must be missions or
something!

[MR. BARNABY *removes the coat, and then climbs to
attend to the star*]

MRS. THORNBURY

We didn't hope to see *you* here, Mr. Goodkind.

MRS. TICE

I met him in front of Tiffany's!

JERRY

The most dangerous corner in New York!

MRS. TICE

And lured him here by mentioning that Clare Jewett was helping us.

DILLY

Somebody page Mr. Gilchrist!

MRS. GILLIAM

Dilly! What a way of saying that Clare is engaged to the assistant rector! . . . Dilly's looking well today, isn't she, Mr. Goodkind? So young, and——

JERRY

And fresh.

DILLY

Oh, boy!

MRS. TICE

Do come and see what I've got for the girls of the Bible Class!

MRS. THORNBURY

Testaments?

MRS. TICE

That's just it; I *haven't!* Bibles are so bromidic! I want to give them something they can *really use!* And it's so hard to think of presents for those girls; they've got everything! [*Opening a small parcel she has withheld from* MR. BARNABY] Guess how I've solved the problem!

MRS. THORNBURY

I can't!

MRS. GILLIAM

I haven't an idea!

DILLY

I'm dying to know!

MRS. TICE

[*Impressively. Displaying the gift*]: Sterling silver vanity cases!

DILLY

[*Taking it*]: How ducky!

MRS. THORNBURY

Charming!

MRS. GILLIAM

An inspiration!

DILLY

[*Showing it to* JERRY]: All complete—lip-stick, powder and some nice, red rouge.

JERRY

[*Cynically*]: To put on before you pray?

DILLY

Precisely. To put on—before we—*prey!*

MRS. THORNBURY

[*Gathering up her coat*]: Well, good people, this is where I leave you!

MRS. GILLIAM

[*With the air of one bereft*]: Oh, Mrs. Thornbury!

MRS. THORNBURY

I've done my "one kind deed" today, and I've an engagement for dinner.

JERRY

Permit me. [*Helping her.*] Some coat!

MRS. THORNBURY

Yes . . . thanks. . . . See you all tomorrow at the Christmas Service! Good-bye, everybody! And Mr. Goodkind! Miss *Jewett's* wrapping things in the choir room! [*Everybody laughs. She exits L.*]

MR. BARNABY

I'll just try those lights. [*Exits L.*]

MRS. GILLIAM

She has an engagement for dinner, but you notice she didn't say with whom! I don't think they ought to allow divorced women in the church!

MRS. TICE

[*Virtuously*]: The church *won't* marry them!

MRS. GILLIAM

That's the trouble!

DILLY

[*Indicating*]: The church *will* let 'em give stained glass windows!

MRS. GILLIAM

Where does she get all her money?

MRS. TICE

Billy settled for thirty-six thousand a year!

JERRY

[*With growing amusement*]: Think of getting thirty-six thousand a year out of munitions! . . . Gee, what a lot of lives that coat must have cost!

[*Everybody laughs, and, on the laugh, enter* DR. WADHAM. *He is* not *the stage clergyman. On the contrary, he is a very pleasant and plausible person—plausible because he believes implicitly in himself. He has passed sixty, and has a really kind heart. But he has had no experience with life, and he has never been uncomfortable.*]

DILLY

[*Hearing the door closed, looks around. Surprised*]: Here's Dr. Wadham!

MRS. GILLIAM

Why, Doctor!

MRS. TICE

We didn't know you were back.

JERRY

I didn't know you'd been away, Doctor.

DR. WADHAM

[*Shakes hands*]: Ten days; attending a Conference on the Proper Use of Eucharistic Candles. It's a subject on which I feel *rather* strongly. [*Turns R.*] It's pleasant to see you, Mrs. Tice. And Miss Daffodil.

MRS. GILLIAM

Isn't Dilly looking *wonderful?*

DR. WADHAM

Quite wonderful! [*Glancing at the tree*] And what a beautiful tree! The star lights up, I suppose.

DILLY

Well, we have hopes!

DR. WADHAM

Don't let me interrupt. I've only dropped in to keep an appointment with the wardens.

MRS. GILLIAM

We're all through, except for putting these gifts under the tree. [*She busies herself with that task*] Miss Jewett will be in with hers any minute. [JERRY, *who has been contemplating an excursion to the choir room, returns from the door, and helps* MRS. GILLIAM] The star is *real* imitation diamonds. A gift from Mrs. Tice.

MRS. TICE

[*Joining* DR. WADHAM *L.C.*]: Speaking of gifts, Doctor——

DR. WADHAM

Yes, dear lady.

MRS. TICE

My husband wanted me to have a little talk with you about his check.

[*She pauses for encouragement, finding what she has been told to say a trifle difficult*] You know, he promised five thousand dollars to beautify the parlor of the Parish House.

DR. WADHAM

[*Foreseeing trouble*]: Oh, yes.

Mrs. Tice

And since then—well, frankly, Doctor, John was very much upset about last Sunday's sermon. Mr. Gilchrist preached from the text about the rich man entering the Kingdom of Heaven.

Dr. Wadham

Always a trifle dangerous.

Mrs. Tice

Yes, and last Sunday it seemed as if he were directing *all* his remarks at John. We're in the first pew, you know, and John says he doesn't like to complain, but there's getting to be altogether too much of this— Bolshevism. John says the preachers are more than half to blame for the present social unrest. I heard the sermon, and I agree with John that some of it was positively insulting!

Dr. Wadham

Mr. Gilchrist is young.

Jerry

Mr. Gilchrist is a nut!

Mrs. Tice

Do you know what he said, Doctor? He said all this —"decking the church"—was making an accomplice of God. He said we couldn't take credit to ourselves for returning a small portion of our *ill-gotten gains!*

Mrs. Gilliam

Small portion! When I've just given away five hundred pounds of coffee!

Mrs. Tice

He said charity wasn't giving away what you didn't want!

Mrs. Gilliam

It was *good* coffee, too! Our second best coffee!

Mrs. Tice

Of course, what John objected to was the reference to rents—to charging clerks and bookkeepers more than they could pay for "wretched little flats." John says he doesn't come here to be told how to run his business!

Mrs. Gilliam

Quite right! And I don't pay seven thousand dollars a year to hear my husband's coffee roasted!
[*They all laugh—the more because of the previous tension.* Mrs. Gilliam, *surprised at first, sees the point, and joins in the laughter*.]
Well, you understand what I mean!

Dr. Wadham

We understand, Mrs. Gilliam.

Mrs. Gilliam

Personally, I'm very fond of Mr. Gilchrist. His father had stock in our stores. But I *don't* think he's a good influence. This used to be a really *exclusive* church. Now, whenever Mr. Gilchrist preaches, there's such a crush of undesirable people in the galleries you can hardly get to your pew. We don't have that trouble with Dr. Wadham!

[CLARE JEWETT *enters R., her arms full of parcels.*
CLARE *is 28. Smartly dressed, though in a fashion
that suggests thought rather than expenditure,
and pretty, in spite of a certain hardness. The
next sentence arrests her, and she stands in the
doorway; not eavesdropping, but not interrupting.*]

MRS. TICE
Mr. Gilchrist was such a promising young man!

MRS. GILLIAM
So rich, and happy!

DILLY
[*Tantalizing* JERRY]: And in love!

DR. WADHAM
He's still rich, and in love, and, I think, he's still
happy.

JERRY
I've told you; he's a nut!

MRS. GILLIAM
I wonder if that's it. Don't laugh! He wasn't like
this before he went overseas as chaplain. Is it possible
he was *gassed*—or something?

CLARE
Here's another armful of presents.

DR. WADHAM
Oh, how do you do, Miss Jewett?

CLARE

I'm very well, thank you.

JERRY

[*Starting to her*]: Hello, Clare! This is a——

MRS. GILLIAM

[*Intercepting him C.*]: Surprise! Ha! **And you've been** waiting for her half an hour!

CLARE

[*To* MRS. GILLIAM]: I'm afraid we'll have **to get** Mr. Barnaby. There are so many packages.

DR. WADHAM

Can't I help?

CLARE

Will you, Doctor? And Mr. Hinkle's in there praying for someone to consult about the Christmas music.

DR. WADHAM

I told Mr. Hinkle the choir'd better begin by singing, "Peace, Perfect Peace, With the Loved Ones Far Away."
[DILLY *laughs and turns up L., chanting "My Wife's Gone to the Country." Scandalized,* MRS. GILLIAM *hushes her.*]

MRS. TICE

And, Doctor! About the Parish House . . . shall I tell my husband you'll speak to Mr. Gilchrist?

Dr. Wadham

Yes, I think you may even tell him that's why we're here today. [*He exits R.*]

Mrs. Gilliam

Dilly, *do* hurry!

Mrs. Tice

Can't I drive you home?

Mrs. Gilliam

Thank you so much! Good-bye, Miss Jewett. Good-bye, Mr. Goodkind. We must arrange for you to come up to dinner as soon as the holidays are over. [*He bows*] Dilly, say "good-bye" to Mr. Goodkind!

Dilly

Goodbye-ee!

[Mr. Barnaby *re-enters L. The door closing attracts* Mrs. Gilliam]

Mrs. Gilliam

Oh, Mr. Barnaby, how about the lights?

Mr. Barnaby

I think the trouble's outside.

Mrs. Gilliam

You'll be sure to fix it? [Mr. Barnaby *nods.*]

Mrs. Tice

And will you put us in the car? [Mr. Barnaby *nods again, and goes L.*] I rather dread that mob at the door. [*She follows, groping in her bag for a bill to*

give Mr. Barnaby] Good-bye, Mr. Goodkind . . .
and Miss Jewett, and, if I don't see you tomorrow, a
Merry, *Merry* Christmas!

[*There is a chorus of repetitions of this wish, amid
which exeunt* Mrs. Tice, Mrs. Gilliam, Dilly *and*
Mr. Barnaby.]

Clare

It's funny to find you in church.

Jerry

Why? My father's the senior warden.

Clare

[*Laughs and takes up a parcel*]: Whatever else you
inherit, Jerry, it's not likely to be religion!

Jerry

Religion doesn't trouble the old man much—except
Sundays. I came here to see you.

Clare

Why?

Jerry

You've been avoiding me.

Clare

Nonsense! Come help me with these parcels.

Jerry

I want to talk to you.

Clare

That's just it, Jerry. You always want to talk to
me, and always to say something I don't want to hear.

JERRY

Why not?

CLARE

[*Simply, but not very surely*]: I'm in love with some-one else!

JERRY

You're *what*?

CLARE

[*Looking defiantly into the mocking face quite close to hers and, this time, with conviction*]: I'm in love with someone else!

JERRY

You're in love with Clare Jewett!

CLARE

You're very rude. I'm *engaged* to Mr. Gilchrist, and he loves me, and believes in me, and your sense of de-cency and fair play . . .

JERRY

Inherited from my father?

CLARE

. . . should keep you from proposing to a woman who's going to marry . . .

JERRY

You're not going to marry Mr. Gilchrist. [*He lounges against the ladder.*] What's the use bluffing? We've known each other since childhood. You know I'm not going to give up anything I want because it belongs to somebody else. And I know you're not going to give up what *you* want—comfort and luxury—for a crazy man who wears his collar hind-side before!

CLARE

Jerry!

JERRY

Now that's admitted, let's go on.

CLARE

Mr. Gilchrist isn't exactly poverty-stricken!

JERRY

No; he got quite a lot of money from his father. You like him and when you said "yes," you thought you were getting somebody you liked, and all the rest of it, too. But something's gone wrong with Gilchrist, and you know it!

CLARE

Why do you say that?

JERRY

Because, if you didn't before, you heard this afternoon. I saw you standing in the door. And I'm going to tell you a few things more!

CLARE

I don't want to listen!

JERRY

Maybe—but you will! Do you know that your young trouble-hunter has given away nearly one-tenth of his capital in three months?

CLARE

No, and I don't believe it!

JERRY

All right; ask my father! The old man has his money in trust! Gilchrist won't touch his income from Gilliam Groceries, because they're profiteering, and he's preaching such anarchy that both wardens are coming this afternoon to complain to Dr. Wadham! I don't want you to throw yourself away on a raving bug!

CLARE

And your advice is——

JERRY

Marry me. I'm a nice fellow, too—and I can give you what you really care about. You're over your ears in debt, without any chance of paying up—or cutting down. And you are, shall we say, twenty-nine in October? I know what it cost you when your father died, and you had to come down a peg. You don't want to keep on—coming down, *do* you?

CLARE

And so—you advise me to marry *you*?

JERRY

Yes.

CLARE

[*Looking at him squarely and significantly*]: Knowing all I *do* know about you?

JERRY

I don't see how *that* concerns you.

CLARE

It proves you don't love me.

JERRY

I want you, and I'm offering marriage to get you.

CLARE

You haven't said one word of love.

JERRY

I've said: "What's the use bluffing?" I'm no movie hero—and no crazy dreamer. I'm a little shop-worn, perhaps—maybe, a little soiled—but I'm sane, and I'm solvent. You're good-looking, and smart, and a lady. You'll help my standing and I'll help your credit. For the rest—we needn't bother each other too much. . . . What do you say?

CLARE

I say it's—*revoltingly*—sordid!

JERRY

[*Looks at her an instant*]: All right! [*Takes out his watch, looks at that, and crosses to L.*] You think it's sordid at 3.45 on Christmas Eve. Well, keep your ears and your mind open, and see how you feel in the morning. My telephone's six nine four two Rhinelander—and this is the last time I shall ask you! [*Puts his hand on the knob*].

CLARE

Wait! [*He turns back*] Whatever you believe of me, I love Mr. Gilchrist!

JERRY

Rhinelander six nine four two.

CLARE

And, what's more, I'm going to marry him!

JERRY

Rhinelander six nine four two.

CLARE

Jerry, I think you're the most detestable person I've ever known in my life!

JERRY

[*Laughing*]:   Rhinelander six . . . nine . . . four . . . two!

[*He exits L., leaving* CLARE *humiliated and fuming. She stands still a moment, and then starts to exit R. At the tree, she throws down the parcels she is still carrying, and, as she does so,* DR. WADHAM *re-enters R.*]

DR. WADHAM

Why . . . Miss Jewett!

CLARE

I'm nervous! . . . I want to finish up and go home!

[*She exits R.* DR. WADHAM *looks after her; then picks up the parcels.* JERRY'S *father,* GEORGE GOODKIND, *enters L. He is about the Doctor's age—sixty— but he has had vast experience with life, and he enjoys comfort now because he has been very uncomfortable. Goodkind is much like any other successful business man you might meet—and like —at dinner. He is brisk and economical of time,*

but pleasant, and, unless his interests are in-
volved, extremely amiable. He does what he con-
ceives to be his duty by his family, his community,
and his God, and feels that all three should ap-
preciate it.]

DR. WADHAM

Ah . . . Mr. Goodkind! [*Glances at his watch*]
You're early!

GOODKIND

How do you do, Doctor? [*Puts down his hat*]
Walked out of a meeting. I don't like letting religion
interfere with business, but I wanted to get here before
Benfield. It's about young Gilchrist.

DR. WADHAM

Shall we go into my study?

GOODKIND

Benfield's coming here, and I've only a few minutes.
Did you know Gilchrist proposes to preach a Christmas sermon about the strike?

DR. WADHAM

What strike?

GOODKIND

This garment strike. He announced his subject from
the pulpit, and Benfield's furious.

DR. WADHAM

Mr. Benfield isn't interested in clothing.

GOODKIND

No, but he's invested heavily in my West Virginia coal mines, and down there we're on the verge of the biggest walk-out in our history. You see what I mean?

DR. WADHAM

Yes.

GOODKIND

The labor problem's none of the church's business. Or any outsider's business. It's a worrisome subject, and there's no good stirring it up. That's what you want to tell Gilchrist!

DR. WADHAM

I have told him . . . frequently.

GOODKIND

And what's the answer?

DR. WADHAM

He says every problem ought to be the church's business, and that, until the church becomes a power in live issues, it isn't a power in life!

GOODKIND

He won't listen to reason?

DR. WADHAM

No.

GOODKIND

Then he'll have to listen to something else. If he persists about this Christmas sermon—[BARNABY *enters* L. GOODKIND *turns. Impatiently*] What is it, Barnaby?

MR. BARNABY

There's a man out there wants to see **Mr. Gilchrist.**

GOODKIND

What kind of a man?

MR. BARNABY

[*Indifferently*] : A poor man.   I think he's a Jew.

GOODKIND

Who ever heard of a poor Jew?

DR. WADHAM

Mr. Gilchrist isn't here.

MR. BARNABY

I told him that, but he won't go away.   I wanted to
ask had I better send for the police?

DR. WADHAM

Oh, I wouldn't do that!

MR. BARNABY

Why don't he go over to the Synagogue instead of
hanging around a Christian Church?   Mr. Gilchrist
gave this fellow his overcoat.   I suppose he's come back
for the gloves!

DR. WADHAM

Tell him I'll speak to Mr. Gilchrist.   [MR. BARNABY
shakes his head despairingly and exits.]

GOODKIND

Well, there you are, and what I wanted to talk about
privately is . . . what's got into the boy?   Has he
gone crazy?

Dr. Wadham

I've asked myself that. I've asked myself if what he saw in France——

Goodkind

Exactly. A lot of young fellows go off the handle and start out to reform the world, but this lad has run through twenty thousand dollars in less than three months!

Dr. Wadham

In addition to his salary?

Goodkind

Yes. I could understand if he'd spent the money on himself, but he hasn't! He's given it away! [Dr. Wadham *shakes his head*] Gilchrist's father was my first partner, and I got the boy in here, and I feel responsible for him. As trustee, I can refuse to turn over another penny of his principal, and, as senior warden, I can demand his resignation from this church. But I want him to have every chance. Tell him if he'll get a grip on himself, and reconsider tomorrow's sermon——[*Enter* Benfield *L.*] Here's Benfield!

[*"Charlie" Benfield is fifty, and a "rough diamond." He is self-made, and proud of it, though nothing really good—nothing of education, or refinement, or knowledge and appreciation of fine things—has gone into the making. He is arrogant, domineering, used to having his own way, and to sweeping aside obstacles. He comes in with his hat on his head, and it is a minute later, when* Dr. Wadham's

*glance makes him aware of the fact, that he re-
moves it.*]

BENFIELD

Hello, George! Howd'y', Doctor! Am I late?

DR. WADHAM

[BENFIELD'S *very presence makes him nervous*]:
We've been waiting for you. Hadn't we better retire
to my study if we're going to discuss Mr. Gilchrist?

BENFIELD

We're not! We've been discussing long enough! All
I got to say now is: Gilchrist leaves this church or
I do!

GOODKIND

Now wait a minute!

DR. WADHAM

Isn't that a little mandatory?

BENFIELD

I don't know what it is, but it goes! I've worked
hard all my life, and now this fellow gets up and tells
me what I've worked for is nothing, and that I'm nothing, and all my ideas is wrong!

DR. WADHAM

He didn't say that.

BENFIELD

Oh, yes, he did—last Sunday and every Sunday!
I've got two million dollars tied up in Black River
mines, and I'm not paying to have the socialist papers
down there print that my own minister is in favor of
strikes!

GOODKIND

Wait a minute, Charlie! That's not the tone to take to Dr. Wadham! We all feel that Gilchrist has gone too far, and we're agreed——

BENFIELD

Does he preach tomorrow?

GOODKIND

We're agreed that if he insists on preaching about the strike——

BENFIELD

He goes?

GOODKIND

He goes!

BENFIELD

All right. And if he don't insist?

GOODKIND

He stays.

BENFIELD

And I go! [*He gets his hat and returns.* DANIEL GILCHRIST *enters L.*] You can decide which of us is the most valu'ble to your church! Because I tell you again—and straight—this church ain't big enough for Gilchrist and me!

DANIEL

[*Smiling*]: A church that isn't big enough for two little men, Mr. Benfield, must be somewhat crowded for God!

[BENFIELD *cannot trust himself to answer. He jams his hat upon his head, and exits L.* GILCHRIST *is 33. He was a football hero at college, and shows it. He was a gentleman before he went to college, and he has been one ever since, and he shows that, too. What he doesn't show is what one expects in a "reformer"—narrowness, hardness, something forbidding. An ascetic, beyond doubt, self-denial has only made him trim and fit. The goodness that shines in his face is partly good humor. He has honest eyes, with fire in them, and there is strength and zeal back of that—strength and zeal that will leave their mark later. As yet, his exaltation is chiefly in his smile. His great gift is charm—and sympathy. At this moment, he wears no overcoat, and is glowing from the cold. Still smiling, he looks after* BENFIELD.]

DR. WADHAM

[*Embarrassed*]: Mr. Benfield is a little—ah—a little——

DANIEL

Yes; a little.

[GOODKIND *crosses for his hat, and observes* DANIEL, *who is chafing his wrists.*]

GOODKIND

Pneumonia weather, Daniel! Where's your overcoat?

DANIEL

Outside.

GOODKIND

Oh, yes. There's a man out there, too, who says he won't go 'way until he sees you. [*He joins* DANIEL] Dan, you're an awfully decent fellow, but I still think you made a mistake going into the church. If you ever want to talk it over with me, I'd be glad to help you— any time! You know that! Good-bye, Doctor! Good-bye, Dan, and a Merry Christmas! [*He exits L.*]

DR. WADHAM

Daniel, you're in trouble.

DANIEL

[*Smiling*]: Doctor, I'm used to it.

DR. WADHAM

This time it's serious. I've warned you often. I don't see how you can have been so blind.

DANIEL

I haven't been blind.

DR. WADHAM

Then you don't care for your position in this church.

DANIEL

[*With feeling*]: There's only one thing I care for more.

DR. WADHAM

And that is?

DANIEL

To be worthy of it.

DR. WADHAM

When you're as old as I am, Daniel, you'll understand that being honest doesn't necessarily mean being disagreeable.

DANIEL

Doesn't it mean—telling the truth?

DR. WADHAM

Do you know the truth, Daniel?

DANIEL

Yes; don't you? Doesn't every man—in his heart? And if we want to keep it in our hearts, and never think about it or look it in the face, shouldn't someone pry open the door and cry: "Behold"? . . . I didn't tell them anything they didn't know, Doctor. I don't *know* anything they don't know. I just reminded them——

DR. WADHAM

[*Exploding on the last word*]: That we were heathen!

DANIEL

That we were Christians, and every man our brother, and that we were sitting, overdressed and overfed, in a Christian Church, while our brother froze and starved —outside—in a Christian World!

DR. WADHAM

That isn't fair! These good people have given——

DANIEL

Given—what cost them nothing! Frumpery and trumpery and diamond stars! That's how all of us give —what we don't need; what we don't even want! . . . You're a good man, Doctor, and, honestly, what would you say tomorrow if your wife told you she'd sold her rings, and given the money to the poor?

Dr. Wadham

Why, I——

Daniel

You'd say she was crazy!

Dr. Wadham

But there's no necessity——

Daniel

Oh, yes, there is! There'll be people lying in the parks tonight. What would Mrs. Tice say if I invited them to sleep in her pew?

Dr. Wadham

That there's no reason why she should share dirt and disease!

Daniel

Exactly! We may *believe* in the brotherhood of man, but we *know* about germs! We're not sure what is truth, but there's one thing we *are* sure of, and *mean* to be sure of, and that's our own comfort! You know that, and I know it, and they know it—but we mustn't say it! All right; in God's name, what *are* we to say?

Dr. Wadham

[*Who has been nervously regarding this raving as confirming the worst fears of* Mr. Goodkind]: Precisely. And that brings us to tomorrow's sermon. I understand you intend to talk about the strike. [*Dan nods "Yes"*] And that's not a very pleasant subject for Christmas. Wouldn't it be more fitting to preach from the text, "Glory to God in the Highest"?

Daniel

"And on earth, Peace, good will toward men"?

Dr. Wadham

[*Delighted*] : Yes! You might say, "There are many kinds of peace——"

Daniel

But there aren't!

Dr. Wadham

There is physical peace—peace that came with the end of this cruel war!

Daniel

There *is* no peace! There is only fear—and hate—and vanity—and lust, and envy, and greed—of men and nations! There are only people preying on one another, and a hungry horde at the very doors of your church! . . . My text will be: "And Peter followed afar off."

Dr. Wadham

I don't understand.

Daniel

[*Into his tone, hitherto indignantly human, comes something mystic—something divine*] : We all follow —afar off.

Dr. Wadham

[*Alarmed; not at the words, but at that "something divine"*] : Daniel . . . my dear fellow!

DANIEL

Don't worry. I'm quite sane. Only—I've been wondering about that for a long time.

DR. WADHAM

Wondering?

DANIEL

What would happen if anybody really tried to live like Christ.

DR. WADHAM

[*Shaking his head*]: It can't be done.

DANIEL

Isn't it worth trying? Men risk their lives—every day—in experiments far less worth while. We've had centuries of "fear, and hate, and greed"—and where have they brought us? Why not try love?

DR. WADHAM

How can you make them try?

DANIEL

By showing that it would work.

DR. WADHAM

It *won't* work, Daniel. It's a beautiful ideal, but it won't work. Times have changed, and things are different. Life isn't as simple as it was two thousand years ago. The trouble with you, Daniel, is that you're not practical.

DANIEL

I wonder.

Dr. Wadham

And the great need of the church is practical men. We mustn't take the Scriptures too literally. We must try to interpret their spirit. And, above all, we must please our congregations, or we shan't have any. And then what becomes of our influence? Better fall back on my text for tomorrow, Daniel.

Daniel

I can't.

Dr. Wadham

At least, you must promise not to discuss the strike.

Daniel

I can't do that, Doctor.

Dr. Wadham

Or else let me take the pulpit.

Daniel

I won't do that! [*A pause.*]

Dr. Wadham

Very well! Preach your Christmas sermon, and afterward——

Daniel

Yes?

Dr. Wadham

I think you may find a greater field of usefulness elsewhere. [*A long pause. The men look at each other, and then* Daniel *turns away to conceal his emotion. He goes up for his hat, and returns.*] I'm sorry, Daniel. I know you've been very happy in your work here. I know how failure hurts. But you saw it coming, and you wouldn't turn aside.

DANIEL

[*He looks up with flashing eyes*]: The man who turns away from his vision—lies! [*Shakes hands*] It's all right, Doctor. [*He crosses L.* CLARE JEWETT, *ready for the street, enters R.*]

DR. WADHAM

[*Brightly*]: Well, Miss Jewett! [DANIEL *hears the name and stops. He is consoled by her very presence*] What's happened to the choir?

CLARE

Mr. Hinkle cut his finger. I've been applying first aid.

DR. WADHAM

Woman's traditional mission—to bind our wounds. [*He turns to exit, and sees* DANIEL. *He is struck by the double significance of his remark, and the timeliness of* CLARE's *arrival.*]

Well, I must be going! Step into my study in the morning, Daniel, and we'll have a look at your sermon! [*He exits L. From here the lights dim very slowly.*]

CLARE

I hope I never see another doll! Got anything on your mind, Dan?

DANIEL

[*Quickly*]: What do you——

CLARE

I mean anything special to do?

DANIEL

Oh!—No.

CLARE

Take me home.

DANIEL

[*He beams*]: *I'm* getting *my* Christmas present early! [*Gets his hat.*]

CLARE

Where's your coat?

DANIEL

Outside. That is—I lent it to a friend. Oh, I've got another—somewhere!

CLARE

But you can't go out without a coat. [*Looks at wrist watch*] Anyway, I told the taxi man to come back at half past four. That's the worst of not having a car. Well, we may as well sit down! [*He assists her, but his mind is afar.*] What's the matter with you, Dan?

DANIEL

Nothing important.

CLARE

There will be if you insist on going around without an overcoat! [*Looking at him narrowly*] You're too generous. [*He is still afar.*]

I say you're too generous! How are we going to be married if you go on giving things away?

DANIEL

[*Laughs*]: Is generosity a fault in a husband?

CLARE

That depends. Is it true you've been giving away—well—large sums of money?

DANIEL

Who told you that?

CLARE

A little bird. [*He laughs*] And that you've refused to take part of your income?

DANIEL

Little bird tell you that?

CLARE

Yes.

DANIEL

Must have been a cuckoo!

CLARE

Is it true?

DANIEL

About the money? Yes.

CLARE

Why?

DANIEL

Well, there's the strike, and a good deal of unemployment, and I've got so much. Why—*I've got you!*

CLARE

[*Rises*]: Let's not talk about it now. [*She turns L. Hesitates; looks at her wrist watch; looks off L.*] Yes; let's!—You're so changed. I hardly know you. We don't seem to want the same things any more.

DANIEL

What do *you* want, Clare?

CLARE

I want to be happy.

DANIEL

That's exactly what I want!

CLARE

How can anybody be happy without money?

DANIEL

How can anybody be happy *with* it? Anyway, do you think people are? Happier than the people who just have enough?

CLARE

In our day and age there's nothing worse than poverty! There's nothing more degrading than having to scrimp, and save, and do without, and keep up appearances! I've tried it . . . ever since my father died . . . and I know! I can't do it any longer, and I won't!

DANIEL

Clare!

CLARE

[*She turns away, and comes back somewhat calmer*]: I don't want to quarrel with you, Dan. I just want you to be sensible . . . I love you, but I love the good things of life, too. I like to be warm and comfortable.

DANIEL

You can be sure of that.

CLARE

But that's only the beginning. I want good clothes, and furs, and my car, and money to spend when I like. I want my own house, and my own servants, and

a husband who amounts to something. **I'm no different**
from other women of my class.

Daniel

I hoped you were.

Clare

A year or two ago people thought **you were going**
to be a Bishop. Today you've made an enemy of every
influential man in the church. All that may be very
noble, but I'm not noble, and I don't pretend to be. I
don't feel any call to sacrifice myself for others, and I
don't think you have any right to ask it!

Daniel

I do ask it, Clare.

Clare

You mean you're going on like this?

Daniel

I mean I can't give you expensive clothes, and servants, and a big house while all about us people are
hungry.

Clare

What do you propose to give me?

Daniel

A chance to help.

Clare

To help wash the dishes, I suppose, in a three-room
flat in a side street!

Daniel

And to visit the sick, and befriend the friendless.

Clare

A charming prospect!

DANIEL

It really is, Clare. You don't know how happy we can be with work, and our modest plenty. There's so much to do—and they won't let me do it here. We've got to get *near* the people in trouble, and we can't with a big house and all that. I don't think we shall come to a three-room flat. [*He smiles*] We'll have five or six rooms, and our books, and each other.

CLARE

I can't believe you're serious. You've always been a dreamer, but I can't believe you're going through with this fantastic nonsense!

DANIEL

I've chosen a narrow path, dear, but I hoped it might be wide enough for us both.

CLARE

It isn't. With your means and opportunities, you're offering me what any bank clerk would give his wife. I thought you loved me, but you're utterly selfish, and I think a little mad. You've a right to throw away your own life, but you've no right to throw away mine. [*She hands him his ring*] Our engagement is off. [*A pause. She starts for the door, and then hesitates, looks at her wrist watch, waits for him to call her back. When he doesn't, she returns.*] Don't you think you're making a terrible mistake?

DANIEL

[*Looks up from the ring. Simply*]: No. [CLARE *turns again, this time quickly and with resolution, and exits L. The church is quite dark, except for light streaming from the open door R. Dan looks at the ring, and puts it in his pocket. With his back to the audience, he looks at the altar of his church. Suddenly, from R., the organ is heard, playing "Hark the Herald Angels." He crosses and closes the door. In the blackness, he hears a step. The Poor Man has come on through the open door L.]* Who's there? . . . Are you looking for someone?

Poor Man

Yes.

Daniel

I'm the assistant rector . . . Mr. Gilchrist.

Poor Man

I know you, Mr. Gilchrist.

Daniel

Oh, yes; I remember. You're the man who was cold. Can I do anything for you?

Poor Man

I think you can.

Daniel

Let's have it then.

Poor Man

Perhaps I can help you, too.

Daniel

In what way?

Poor Man

In my way.

DANIEL

My poor man, I wish you could!

[*His despair impels him to confide in anyone*]: I was so sure of what I wanted to do, and now I begin to wonder if it can be done!

POOR MAN

It has been done.

DANIEL

But in this day—in this practical world—can any man follow the Master?

POOR MAN

Why not? Is this day different from any other? Was the world never practical before? Is this the first time of conflict between flesh and spirit? If it could be done then, why not now, and, if it was ever worth the doing, why not now?

DANIEL

But how?

POOR MAN

We have been told how.

DANIEL

"Take no thought of the morrow. . . . Sell whatsoever thou hast, and give to the poor. . . . Love thy neighbor as thyself. . . . Bless them that curse you, do good to them that hate you." But if a man did those things today people would think him mad!

POOR MAN

What does it matter?

DANIEL

He would lose everything!

L. An instant later, GOODKIND, *in evening clothes, enters L. He has a card in his hand. The* SERVANT *re-enters, re-crosses, and re-exits, stopping, en route, to switch on the lights.* GOODKIND *looks at the pile on the table, and turns the topmost paper face down.* BENFIELD, *also in evening clothes, enters L.*

BENFIELD

What the h—

GOODKIND

Shut the door.

[BENFIELD *does so. As he returns,* GOODKIND *gives him the card*]

BENFIELD
[*Reading*]

"Labor conciliators."

[*Throws the card on the table*]

What the h—

GOODKIND

What are labor conciliators? Mostly thugs. When you've been director in a coal mining company a little longer you'll know. We've got a million dollars' worth of 'em handling this strike.

BENFIELD

Police duty?

GOODKIND

No; spies and agents provocateur. I hate the breed, but what are you going to do about it? This fellow, Max Stedtman, got into the union five or six years ago, and now he's one of the delegation they've sent up to me. . . . Where's Jerry?

BENFIELD

I gave him the high sign.

GOODKIND
[*Offering cigars*]:

Smoke?

BENFIELD
[*Taking one*]:

Thanks. . . . Why didn't you go down to West Virginia?

GOODKIND

Had to look over that power plant in Canada.

BENFIELD

Oh, yes!

GOODKIND

Anyway, what do I know about coal mining?

BENFIELD

You're president of the company.

GOODKIND

Yes, but that means digging up money—not coal. I've never set foot in West Virginia in my life; and I don't want to!

BENFIELD

Yes, but in a serious situation like this—

GOODKIND

I sent Jerry. Jerry has a dozen qualifications and no scruples. *And* I sent Gilchrist.

BENFIELD

Who has scruples and no qualifications.

GOODKIND

Thus striking a balance. I mean that! Don't make any mistake about Gilchrist. He's a valuable man. I didn't hire him because I was sorry he got fired out of the church . . . and only a little because I knew his father. I hired him because he had theories, and I wanted to try 'em out!

BENFIELD

I'll say he's got theories!

GOODKIND

Yes, and the remarkable part of it is . . . sometimes they work. They worked up at that power plant. A year ago I wouldn't have taken it as a gift. Gilchrist applied a little soft soap—

BENFIELD

Soft soap or gold dust?

GOODKIND

Well, both; but, damn it, Charlie, with all the increased wages and decreased working hours, the plant's making money now for the first time!

[*Enter* JERRY L. *He is a little sullen—the result of brandy and resentment. He, too, is in evening clothes, and he closes the door behind him.*]

GOODKIND

There's something *in* Gilchrist!

JERRY

Mostly bugs!

GOODKIND

All right!

JERRY

I told you what he was doing at the mines. Now he wires you, "Everything settled if you accede to rational conditions," and up comes this delegation! What are the conditions? I'll tell you now—surrender! You're crazy if you see these workmen! We've nothing to discuss! They're our mines, and we'll run 'em as we like! If this philanthropist of yours carries out instructions we've got 'em whipped! . . . What was the idea of the high sign?

GOODKIND

[*As* BENFIELD *picks up the card to answer*]: Stedtman.

JERRY

Where?

GOODKIND

On the way up.

JERRY

Of course, we're leaving our guests flat!

BENFIELD

Your wife's in there!

JERRY

Clare resents our talking business at home.

GOODKIND

Resents—and you haven't been married a year! Palaver's a wife's job! They oil the machinery while we shovel in coal! [*The* SERVANT *re-enters R.*]

SERVANT

Mr. Stedtman.

[*Enter* MAX STEDTMAN. *He is a wiry little man, with
    the face of a ferret and the furtiveness of a rat.
    His nervousness does not indicate lack of self-
    confidence. That quality has made Stedtman the
    man he is to-day. For the rest, he is 40, and
    faintly Semitic. The* SERVANT *exits.*]

GOODKIND

How do, Stedtman? This is Mr. Benfield—one of
our new directors.

   [*They acknowledge the introduction*]
You know my son.

STEDTMAN

[*Nods*] : Saw him down to Black River.

[*They sit*—JERRY *down L.;* BENFIELD *left of the
    table;* GOODKIND *back of it;* STEDTMAN *R.*]

GOODKIND

Well?

STEDTMAN

Well . . . the committee's on its way.

GOODKIND

Who's in this delegation?

STEDTMAN

I'm chairman. We got a Pole called Umanski.

GOODKIND
   [*Writes*] :

Umanski.

STEDTMAN

He's a radical. You can't do anything with him.
But there's a fellow named Joe Hennig . . .

GOODKIND

Who'll listen to reason?

STEDTMAN

I think so.

GOODKIND

Why?

STEDTMAN

He's got a pretty wife.

BENFIELD

What the he——

GOODKIND

What has that to do with it?

STEDTMAN

Lots. Pretty wives like pretty things. Hennig's in
debt, and this girl's on his neck every minute. She's
a peach. You know her, Mr. Jerry!

JERRY

No.

STEDTMAN

Pearl Hennig?

JERRY

No.

STEDTMAN

Oh! I thought I saw you talking to her onct. Anyhow, Gilchrist knows her . . . *well*.

BENFIELD

You mean . . .

STEDTMAN

I mean I wouldn't mention Gilchrist to Joe Hennig.
[BENFIELD whistles.]

GOODKIND

That's rot!

STEDTMAN

Anyhow, Hennig and me are two votes, and I figure
Hennig's'll cost about . . .

[*He looks at them narrowly.*]

. . . fifteen thousand dollars.

[*All three show surprise.*]

GOODKIND

I don't like bribery.

BENFIELD

Not when it isn't necessary.

GOODKIND

And Gilchrist wired yesterday: "Everything settled."

JERRY

On conditions.

STEDTMAN

Yeh—on *their* conditions! Take it from me, this
Gilchrist has double-crossed you!

BENFIELD

I told you!

JERRY

He's a . . .

STEDTMAN

[*Goes right on, without heeding the simultaneous interruption*]:

He's been at union meetings! *He* got 'em to send this delegation, and he tried to get 'em to turn down Hennig—our one best bet! *You take it from me—*

GOODKIND

[*Quietly*]: I won't take it from you, Stedtman. [*Looks around*] Or from anybody else. I know this man.

STEDTMAN

[*Cowed*]: Well, he's gone around talkin' compromise. Compromise ain't no way to settle a strike. Givin' 'em confidence. Why, we got a couple o' hundred representatives among the workmen tellin' 'em they got no chance. We got special police clubbin' 'em every time they try to hold a meeting. You wouldn't believe what we done down there in the way of harmony!

GOODKIND

It's all been done before.

STEDTMAN

Never no completer! We're workin' the black list and, if a man opens his mouth too wide at a meetin', somebody—he don't know who—tips the gover'ment that he's a "red." We got 'em so they ain't sure of their own brothers. We're postin' bills, in seven languages, saying: "Why should workmen mistrust the company? This is the land of opportunity! America

is calling you—GO BACK TO WORK!" The boss has
a scheme now to start a riot between the Poles and
the Wops! And you know the end o' that! Troops,
and scabs, and machine guns! What stopped it? One
gent that don't know nothin' about harmony, or co-
operation, or nothin'—except hangin' around after a
skirt! If you got to descend to bribery now, don't
blame me! Blame Gilchrist!

BENFIELD

[*Rises; striking the table with his open hand*]: He's
absolutely right!

JERRY

[*Rises*]: Of course, he's right! Wha'd'ya expect
of a man kicked out of his church for Bolshevism?

BENFIELD

He ought to be brought back right now!

GOODKIND

He's coming back—
                    [*Servant enters R.*]
Yes; what is it?

SERVANT

Two men to see Mr. Stedtman.

BENFIELD

Good!

GOODKIND

Bring them in.
                [*Servant exits*]

STEDTMAN

Now look—don't try nothin' before Umanski! Just give us an excuse to vote *right*, and then we'll go out, and get rid of him, and I'll slip back with Hennig! Now then— [*His sharp ears have heard footsteps off R. He strikes a pose*] It's very good of you gentlemen to see us! I was goin' to meet my friends outside— [*The Servant ushers in* UMANSKI *and* JOE HENNIG, *and retires*]—but you been so kind and agreeable— Hello, Joe!

JOE

Hello, Max!

UMANSKI

You said you be on sidewalk.

STEDTMAN

I just really got in myself. This is Mr. Goodkind. He's the President. And a couple o' Directors. Well, now we can get down to business!

[*He sits.* UMANSKI *stares in amazement at his temerity.* UMANSKI *is a giant Pole or Russian. Whatever flesh he ever had has been starved off; he is all bone and brawn. In his face is something strangely like poetry . . . something born of silence and suffering. He is in his best, which does not obliterate the picture of the man in working clothes, his sleeves rolled up over his muscular arms. Hennig is a stocky man of 45—a "grouser." His tone has none of the courage, the dignity, the independence of* UMANSKI'S; *he blusters, emptily, an echo, without much to say, and one guesses he might be made to bluster either way. There is a pause.]*

GOODKIND

Smoke? [*He presents the humidor to* HENNIG, *and* STEDTMAN, *rising, reaches out and helps himself.* GOODKIND *goes on to* UMANSKI, *who doesn't unfold his arms; doesn't even appear to see the box.* GOODKIND *returns, and sets it lower right end of table.]*

JOE

[*Coming down R. of* GOODKIND]: I guess you know all about our grievances.

GOODKIND

I didn't know you had any.

JOE

You didn't know we had any—

BENFIELD

Ah, you fellows are never satisfied!

GOODKIND

You're getting plenty for what you do! What are you complaining about? You've left good jobs to follow a lot of idle, discontented agitators! We've got to win this fight on principle! The work's there! I pay what I can get men for, and not a cent more! Take it or leave it!

JOE

We got to hang together to get anything!

GOODKIND

You're hanging, and what have you got?

[*The piano music in the next room, which ceased during
the scene with* STEDTMAN, *is succeeded now by the
low tones of a violin.* UMANSKI *speaks, in a voice
as unemotional as its owner is stolid.*]

UMANSKI

I work twelve hours—every day . . . thirty years
. . . got nothing.

BENFIELD

Why should you have? An untrained man—

JERRY

You don't even know English!

UMANSKI

How I gonna learn English—work twelve hours a
day?

JERRY

Nobody asked you to take the job! Nobody asked
you to come over here! You're not an American!

UMANSKI

I was American.

JERRY

[*Sneers*]: When?

UMANSKI

When I fight . . . in the war. [*A short pause.*]

JERRY

[*Turning to Goodkind*]: We're not getting anywhere. We've been over this a dozen times!

GOODKIND

What do you want?

UMANSKI

I wanna chance to learn! I wanna chance to live!
I wanna see . . . sun!

JERRY

Wha'd'ya mean—*son?*

GOODKIND   [*Together*]

Your son?

UMANSKI

God's sun. I never see him. Go to mines—him not
up. Work in mines—him not see. Go home—him
gone. Got baby five years ago. Never see *him*. Go
to mines . . . *him* not up. Come back—*him* asleep.
Go home one day—*him* gone.

GOODKIND

Dead?

UMANSKI

My wife say: "Good! Not such many to feed!"

JERRY

When you worked you had enough to eat, didn't you?

UMANSKI

Yes. Work twelve hours a day and got enough to

eat—so can work some more. Always work. Get up—
work—come back—sleep—get up—work. Never got
time to talk to wife—never got time to talk to nobody
—never got nowhere. Never save nothing.

Joe

[*Whining*]: It ain't fair! [Jerry *takes out his
cigarette case.*]

Umanski

That little box—what you pay for him? [*Jerry
turns front, not deigning to answer*] Ah, I know;
gold. You pay more for him than I got from swing pick
thirty years. Me and six families—we live in one house
you own. We got one room upstairs; two down cellar.
Sleep there. Eat—cook—wash upstairs. See nothing
but brick yard, and clothes hang up to dry. Wife—
she carry water from yard. Me—I carry potato peel-
ing out front. Him rot. If I don't like that, I quit—
and starve!

Jerry

You want to live on Fifth Avenue!

Benfield

And *then* you'd find something to kick about!

Umanski

If I don't like other mans will. Other mans take my
job. I got little girl twenty years old. Awful nice
little girl. Got gold hair. Got blue eyes. Her take
sick. She sorry she's sick. She wanna go church. She
ask me: "Pop, buy me new dress for church. Buy me

pretty *pink* dress." Where I get him? We hire doctor once, and he say: "Air—sunshine—milk—eggs!" Where I get air—sunshine—milk—eggs? Got no job. My little girl, she cough, and cough, and one night she die. I tell you we got right to quit! We got right to hang together! We got right to fight—to live—and, by God, we gonna fight—we gonna live—*we gonna—* *BY GOD!*

[*The music stops. In the same short instant, there is a patter of applause; more music—lively this time —and, bursting into the room from L.,* DILLY *runs into* UMANSKI. *She has gold hair; she has blue eyes; and what is more, she has a new dress. It is a "pretty pink dress," too, and its owner wears jewels worth the ransom of a dozen Umanskis.*]

DILLY

[*As she enters*]: Now, look here, Jerry; you're not going to— Oh! I'm sorry! [UMANSKI *looks at her; then covers his face, and, with a great sob, drops into a chair R. C.* STEDTMAN *puts his arm about the man's shoulders.* GOODKIND, *C., stares at him sympathetically.*]

JERRY

You'll have to wait, Dilly.

GOODKIND

Ask the ladies to stay in the drawing room. We'll join them in a few minutes.

DILLY

Yes. . . . Certainly. . . . I'm SO sorry!

[*She exits. A pause.* STEDTMAN, *one arm about* UMANSKI, *uses the other to signal* GOODKIND *to go ahead.* GOODKIND *ignores him.*]

GOODKIND

I think we'd better let this go for tonight.

UMANSKI

[*Rising*]: Oh, no! Me—I'm all right! Excuse!

GOODKIND

You're a little upset, and I have guests. Besides, Gilchrist will be here in half an hour, and I want to talk to him before I say anything definite. Suppose we all meet here tomorrow at noon.

JOE

[*Who has turned down angrily at mention of the name*]: Not Gilchrist!

GOODKIND

No; just we six . . . and, maybe, one or two more of our directors.

STEDTMAN

All right!

UMANSKI

I wanna know what we gonna do—*tonight!*

GOODKIND

We're going to get together. You fellows have got the wrong idea. We're not tyrants, or monsters. We're Christians, and we want to act like Christians. Only . . . we've got to live, too. We've got to have the things we're used to, just as you have. But I think I can promise, if the strike's called off, you men will be kept, and put back just where you were. . . . Ring the bell, Jerry.

[JERRY *does so. A pause.*]

BENFIELD

I guess you don't want me any more.

GOODKIND

No.

BENFIELD

Thanks.

[*Exits L. A pause.*]

GOODKIND

[*To* HENNIG. *Making conversation*]: You live in Black River?

JOE

Yes.

GOODKIND

Married?

JOE

You betcha! Prettiest girl in West Virginia! We only been married a year. I got her in the five-and-ten-cent store. . . . I mean, that's where she was working. She's at her sister's now . . . up to Pittsburg. Left the day before I was elected to come here. [*Proudly*] I sent her a telegram!

GOODKIND

You don't say so! [*To* JERRY] Anything the matter with that bell?

JERRY

The man's busy, I suppose.   I'll show them out.

GOODKIND

If you will. . . . Well, good-night!

[*He shakes hands with* HENNIG, *and with* STEDTMAN, *but, when he comes to* UMANSKI, *that giant is immobile. His slow mind has been thinking out the earlier declaration.*]

UMANSKI

What about this here twelve-hour day?

GOODKIND

We'll consider that after the strike's called off.

UMANSKI

And the twenty-four-hour shift?

GOODKIND

We'll consider that, too.   Meanwhile——you go back just where you were!

UMANSKI

Then what good we gain by strike?

GOODKIND

Nothing's ever gained by quarreling.   You'll find that out some day.

UMANSKI

Some day something be gain!   Some day we gonna win!   *This*——he don't go on always!   *You* see!

JERRY

[*Insolently*]: Are you ready?

UMANSKI

[*As* HENNIG *slips out R.,* UMANSKI *looks at* JERRY *with contempt.*] *You* see! [*Exits R.*]

STEDTMAN

[*Significantly,—in a loud whisper*]: We'll be back later. [*He exits R.*]

JERRY

Swine!

[*He exits R.* GOODKIND, *obviously worried by the interview, goes to the table, and rights the topmost paper. Looks at it. Sits, and examines other papers. The* SERVANT *enters R.*]

SERVANT

Did you ring, sir?

GOODKIND

Half an hour ago.

SERVANT

[*Indicating a box*]: I was signing for this. [GOOD-KIND, *writing, doesn't look up.*] Can I do anything for you, sir?

GOODKIND

Yes. . . . Get me a drink.

[*The* SERVANT *hesitates.* GOODKIND *takes key from pocket and gives it to him. The* SERVANT *unlocks a cellarette, up R., takes out decanter and glasses,*

*relocks the cellarette, comes down L. of table, sets
down the tray, and returns the key.*]

Thanks.   [*The* SERVANT *starts to exit L.*]   And,
Riggs!   [*The* SERVANT *stops up L. C.   Enter*
CLARE *L.*]   If Mr. Stedtman comes back to-night . . .
with one of the other men . . . I'll see them in here.

SERVANT

Very good, sir.   [*To* CLARE]: This package just
came for you, Madam.   [*He gives her the box, and
exits L.   A pause.*]

GOODKIND

Everybody gone?

CLARE

They're all down in the billiard room.   We wanted
to make up a couple of tables at bridge, but, with the
men in here . . . as usual. . . . Where's Jerry?

GOODKIND

I don't know.

CLARE

I've seen him just ten minutes this week.

GOODKIND

He's only been back three hours.

CLARE

Well . . . I wish he wouldn't break up my dinner
parties.

GOODKIND

[*Pushes back papers*]: What have you got there?

CLARE

[*Looking at the box*] : Another . . . substitute . . .

GOODKIND

Substitute, for what?

CLARE

[*As she opens it*] : For my husband's time . . . and love . . . and companionship. [*Holds up a sable scarf*] Sables. [*She gives it to* GOODKIND.]

GOODKIND

[*Looking at it with admiration*] : Mm! You don't seem much surprised.

CLARE

No. . . . Whenever Jerry's been away longer than usual, or done something he's a little ashamed of, there's a box from Cartier or Revillon.

GOODKIND

Must have been a whopper this time!

CLARE

[*Seriously. Wondering*] : Yes. [*She takes the scarf.*]

GOODKIND

Pretty generous husband . . . if you ask *me!*

CLARE

Yes. [*She puts the scarf away.*]

GOODKIND

Upon my word, I don't know what you women want! . . . A man works his heart and soul out to get you things, and still you're not satisfied!

CLARE

Maybe we'd like a little "heart and soul."

GOODKIND

Heart and soul, and what a man trades 'em for! You want your husband to succeed, and give all his attention to you! You want him to have plenty of money, and plenty of time! You're willing to take everything, but you're not willing to pay for it!

CLARE

I suppose everybody *must* pay.

GOODKIND

Surest thing you know! You women are all alike. My poor wife—*she* had everything, and I used to catch her crying in a corner. We never seemed to understand each other . . . after we got *this*. She was a good wife, too, but the best of you never seem to want what you have. . . . Sometimes I think we don't any of us really want what we struggle so hard to get. Sometimes I think we're all wrong! [*He looks at his watch, and rises.*] Well, I guess I'll go downstairs!

CLARE

I wish you would.

GOODKIND

[*Goes to her*]: You're not crying? [*She nods and looks up*] My God! Can you beat it?

CLARE

I'll be down in a minute.

GOODKIND

Tell Riggs—will you?—if any one comes, I'll be . . . talking to Jerry. [*He puts his hand on her shoulder*] And . . . buck up! There are people worse off than we are . . . and it's a great life if you don't weaken!

[*He exits L. CLARE goes C. She puts the box, with its contents, on the table, dries her eyes, and is powdering her nose when DANIEL GILCHRIST opens the door R. He is in business clothes, and starts to retire when he sees CLARE. He would a little rather avoid the interview.*]

CLARE

Come in! I'm just powdering my nose. Does that offend your reverence?

DANIEL

On the contrary; I agree with the man who said, "Put your trust in God, and keep your powder dry." [*They laugh.*]

CLARE

When did you get in?

DANIEL

Half an hour ago.

CLARE

Had dinner?

DANIEL

On the train. I was starved. Thank goodness, they don't charge for dinner by the mile! . . . Riggs said your father-in-law was in here.

CLARE

He'll be up in a moment . . . won't you sit down? We haven't had five minutes together since——

DANIEL

[*Hesitates about remaining.*]

CLARE

I understand you're very happy in your new . . . profession.

DANIEL

[*Sits.*] Yes.

CLARE

You've got . . . everything . . . you want?

DANIEL

No, I haven't everything I want, but I'm happy.

CLARE

My father-in-law says if you settle this strike you're to be—but that's a business secret. [*A pause*] I suppose I might tell you. [*A pause*] He says it'll make you a big man in the company . . . with a tremendous salary. . . . You mustn't give it away!

DANIEL

The secret?

CLARE

The salary . . . I suppose you've got over that . . .
So . . . you don't really seem to have lost anything
by giving up your church.

DANIEL

No. Queer as it seems, sometimes I think I've gained
. . . in opportunity.

CLARE

[*Chiefly to herself*]: Perhaps one *might* have eaten
one's cake and had it, too.

DANIEL

Clare!

CLARE

You frightened me so that night, with the bugaboo
of poverty. Don't you think there might have been a
compromise? Something half way?

DANIEL

Why open wounds that are beginning to heal?

CLARE

Yours seem quite healed.

DANIEL

And you have everything *you* want?

CLARE

Yes.

DANIEL

You see . . . I *was* selfish . . . to ask you to give

up the things that count so much with you for those
that count with me. . . . Afterward, when I knew you
were to be married. . . . I was afraid for you . . .
and I was wrong again. [*He rises*] You're happy
. . . and I'm honestly glad!

CLARE

Are you . . . honestly . . . happy?

DANIEL

Honestly.

CLARE

In just helping others?

DANIEL

In just helping others.

CLARE

I don't understand that.

DANIEL

You will . . . some day.

[JERRY *enters R. He has added two or three brandies
     to a generous allowance at dinner, and though not
     drunk, is sullen and quarrelsome. The more so
     at finding* DANIEL *with* CLARE].

JERRY

Hello, Gilchrist! In early, aren't you? [*Crosses.*]
I didn't mean to interrupt a tête-à-tête!

CLARE

You're not interrupting.

JERRY

Where's father?

CLARE

I thought he was with you.

JERRY

I stopped for refreshments.

CLARE

I see you did.

JERRY

[*Laughs and turns to* DANIEL]: We've been having a genial evening with your delegation. That's why my wife's sore.

CLARE

I'm not "sore." I've been a little lonely.

JERRY

You don't look it! . . . I couldn't help going to Black River! I didn't go for pleasure . . . did I, Gilchrist?

DANIEL

No. There was work, and plenty of it. I was sorry you had to leave when you did.

CLARE

Why, Jerry didn't leave much before you, did he?

JERRY

Just a few——

DANIEL

[*At the same time*]: Only twenty-four hours. . . . He wanted to get back to you.

CLARE

But . . . he's just *got* back. . . . Where have you been, Jerry?

JERRY

Attending to business . . . *of course!*

CLARE

Of course. [*She takes the scarf from the box on the table*] Good night, Dan.

DANIEL

[*Cheerily*]: Good night! [*She starts to door L.*].

JERRY

Oh . . . you *got* the furs!

CLARE

Yes . . . thank you.

JERRY

Don't mention it!

CLARE

I'm very grateful . . . but . . .

JERRY

But what?

CLARE

Never mind. We'll talk about it some other time.

JERRY

We'll talk about it *now!*

DANIEL

I'll go. [*Starts R.*].

JERRY

No, you won't! You made a crack about my leaving twenty-four hours before you did! How do you know when I left? [*To* CLARE] If that's what you're sore about, for heaven's sake, drop it! I'm sorry you've been alone, and I've sent you a handsome gift as an apology!

CLARE

I don't want it. [*She lays down the scarf.*] I don't want to be paid for shutting my eyes to any insulting thing you choose to do!

JERRY

And I don't propose to be made a blackguard before strangers!

CLARE

Dan isn't a stranger. And I don't want to make you a blackguard. Only . . . since you've insisted on the truth . . . Dan, when *did* my husband leave Black River?

DANIEL

I haven't seen him since Thursday.

JERRY

There you have it! He hasn't *seen* me since Thursday! Does it occur to you that may have been because *he* wasn't in Black River?

CLARE

No.

DANIEL

As a matter of fact, I wasn't.

JERRY

Oh! . . . Where were you?

DANIEL

At the mines.

CLARE

Is that the truth?

JERRY

Of course it's the truth! And, if it wasn't, I don't see that you've any right to ask questions! I haven't done anything that 'wasn't in the bargain! I haven't done anything every man doesn't do!

CLARE

Every man . . . perhaps . . . but one!

JERRY

Gilchrist! My God! Now we've got it! If you'd only married him! He's good, because he says so! You ought to've been here a minute ago . . . when the company detective warned us not to mention Gilchrist to Joe Hennig!

DANIEL

You mean——

JERRY

I mean Pearl Hennig!

DANIEL

Pearl Hennig? Why, *you*—you *know* that's not true!

CLARE

I know it's not true!

JERRY

Do you?

STEDTMAN

[*Off R.*]: Say . . . now . . . listen . . . you behave yourself!

JOE

[*Off R.*]: Behave . . . hell!

JERRY

[*Continuing above these voices*]: Ask Stedtman! Ask Hennig! And before you make up your mind where *I* was yesterday, ask where *he* was——

[*Enter* STEDTMAN *and* HENNIG, *followed by the* SERVANT. *There is no dead cue for this entrance. They come on*—STEDTMAN *trying to hold back* HENNIG—*flinging open the door as* HENNIG *says* "Hell!" HENNIG *confronts* GILCHRIST.]

JOE

You—Gilchrist! Where've you got my wife?

DANIEL

I haven't got your wife, Hennig.

JOE

The hell you haven't!

DANIEL

You'd better go, Clare.

JERRY

I want her to stay. [*To the* SERVANT] All right!
[*The* SERVANT *exits*] What's it all about, Stedtman?

STEDTMAN

You can search me! Umanski stuck to us all the
way home. When he left, I went in to have a little
talk with Joe . . . alone. . . . See? There was a
telegram, and he read it, and——

JOE

And came here to ask Gilchrist: Where's my wife?

DANIEL

She told me she was going to her sister's.

JOE

She ain't never been *near* her sister, and you know
it! I just got this from her sister! [*Holds out wire.*
JERRY *snatches it.*] Read it!

JERRY

[*Reading*]: Pearl ain't here. We ain't seen her.
Ain't she home?

DANIEL

Maybe she is.

JOE

You know she ain't! And what if she is . . . now?
I don't want your leavings!

DANIEL

Why do you say that, Hennig?

JOE

Why do I say it? Ain't I seen you down town with her? Ain't I found you with her when I came home unexpected? I knew you was stuck on her, and I warned you to stay away . . . didn't I?

DANIEL

You were mistaken.

JOE

Didn't I warn you?

DANIEL

Yes.

JOE

And you came again . . . didn't you?

DANIEL

Yes.

JERRY

Every man but one!

DANIEL

I went first on your account . . . because they told me you were in debt . . . and why. I "came again" because she asked me to. This disappearance looks queer, I admit, but people *do* get lost, or hurt, and taken to hospitals, and aren't identified.

JOE

[*Half convinced*]: You think——

DANIEL

I think your wife's all right, Joe. I don't think you ought to accuse her publicly until you're sure she's not.

JOE

[*Cries*]: How'm I gonna be sure?

DANIEL

Suppose we ask the police to look for her?

JERRY

[*Turning quickly*]: What's the use of starting a hulla-ba-loo? You don't want the woman accused publicly, but you're willing to spread the news so this man'll be ashamed to go back home. We all know the facts in the case, and the least said about it now the better. [*To* JOE] You've found her out. Let her go . . . and forget it!

CLARE

I don't think he ought to forget it.

JERRY

No?

CLARE

No. I don't think he ought to drop it now . . . until we all know the truth.

DANIEL

Right!

JOE

I want to know the truth! I got to! I been crazy about her! Maybe that's a good idea . . . the police. I *got* to know the truth!

JERRY

[*At bay*]: All right! Stedtman! Where were you yesterday?

STEDTMAN

At the mines.

JERRY

What part of the mines?

STEDTMAN

All over.

JERRY

Did you see Gilchrist?

STEDTMAN

No.

[DANIEL *never takes his eyes off* CLARE. *He watches
her, as the net tightens around him, observing,
with ever-increasing agony, that he is convicted in
her eyes.*]

JERRY

When *did* you see him last?

STEDTMAN

Thursday——Yes, it was Thursday.

JERRY

Where?

STEDTMAN

In Black River.

JERRY

Alone?

STEDTMAN

No.

JERRY

With whom?

STEDTMAN

With Mrs. Hennig.

JOE

I knew it! I'm gonna kill you!

JERRY

No, you're not. You're going to keep quiet. But you wanted the truth, and you've got it. I've known it all along. [*To* CLARE] Now do you think I was lying?

CLARE

I don't know. I don't understand.

JERRY

Oh, yes, you do . . . only you won't admit it!

CLARE

I suppose that's it.

[*She takes her scarf and starts wearily to exit L.*]

DANIEL

Clare! [*She stops*] I don't care what anyone believes but you!

CLARE

[*Turns*]: I'll believe you, Dan, if you'll only explain.

DANIEL

I——

JERRY

I forbid you to speak to my wife!

CLARE

Go on, Dan.

JERRY

I forbid you to speak to my wife!

DANIEL

[*Exploding . . . to* JERRY]: If I hadn't anybody to think about but *you!*

[*They stare at each other . . . close together. Suddenly,* JERRY *lifts his open hand, and strikes* DAN *across the mouth.* DAN *starts to retaliate, but controls himself, opens his clinched hands, and lowers his head.*]

CLARE

[*In almost speechless amazement*]: Dan; you're not going to take that?

DANIEL

I have nothing to say.

CLARE

I didn't think you were a coward. You see, I was wrong about everything.

[*The scarf in her hand, she exits L. A short pause. Suddenly,* JOE, *emboldened by what he has witnessed, certain of* DAN's *cowardice, breaks from* STEDTMAN *and rushes at* GILCHRIST.]

JOE

You'll play around *my* wife, will you? [DANIEL *merely looks at him.*] You will . . . will you? . . . Take that! [*He strikes out.* DANIEL *seizes his wrist, and, with one powerful, dexterous movement, hurls him to the floor*].

DANIEL

[*As* HENNIG *struggles to his feet*]: I hope I didn't hurt you, Joe.

STEDTMAN

[*Looks from* DANIEL *to* JERRY]: My God!

JOE

[*Retreating*]: Don't worry! I'll get *you*! It may be a long time, but I'll get *you*! [*He exits.*]

DANIEL

[*With great kindness*]: Take him home, Stedtman. [STEDTMAN *looks to* JERRY, *who jerks his head toward the door.*]

STEDTMAN

Good-night, Mr. Jerry. Tell your father we'll be around . . . [DANIEL *turns and looks at him. He backs toward the door.*] . . . in . . . the . . . morning!

[*Quick exit. He closes the door, which has been left open by* HENNIG. *The two men look at each other.* JERRY *goes to upper left of table, and pours himself a drink.*]

JERRY

Well, you've made a nice mess of it! Why can't you keep your nose out of other people's business? Why did you have to date my leaving Black River?

DANIEL

Why did you have to get mixed up with Pearl Hennig?

JERRY

I can take what I want out of life!

DANIEL

You can. God says: "Here is the world. Take what you want . . . AND PAY FOR IT!"

JERRY

Rubbish! [*Drinks*] Save your preaching for those that like it! [*Comes down*] And keep away from my wife!

DANIEL

Why?

JERRY

Because you're in love with her! Aren't you?

DANIEL

Yes.

JERRY

Well, you've a hell of a nerve to preach to me about Hennig's wife while you're making a play for mine.

DANIEL

I'm not making a play for yours.

JERRY

No? You expect me to believe that when you admit—— Why did you pull that hero stuff? Why did you keep your mouth shut when I lost my temper? Why did you turn the other cheek?

DANIEL

You wouldn't understand, Jerry.

JERRY

Wouldn't I? Well, *you* understand that I've forbidden you to speak to her and that goes. If you come here again, I'll have the servants throw you out, and I'll tell my father why. [GOODKIND *enters L.*]

DANIEL

Here's your father now.

JERRY

And that's not all I'll do!

[*Lowering his voice*]: Not by a damned sight! [*He wheels about and exits.*]

GOODKIND

[*Taking cigars from humidor*]: Smoke?

DANIEL

Thanks.

GOODKIND

[*Looking off after his son*]: Jerry don't like you much, does he?

DANIEL

Not much.

GOODKIND

[*Lights his cigar*]: Well . . . how are things in Black River?

DANIEL

I think we've got everything settled.

GOODKIND

Fine! Benfield'll be up in a minute, and we'll hear the conditions! [*He sits in an easy chair L.*] Somehow, I knew you'd do it! Jerry says you're a philanthropist, but I knew he was wrong!

DANIEL

Thanks.

GOODKIND

If you've really settled this strike . . . our way . . .
your salary from today is thirty thousand a year!

DANIEL

Thanks . . . again.

GOODKIND

I'm dog-sick of rowing with labor! It's such utter
damned waste! . . . *Excuse* me!

DANIEL

I agree with you!

GOODKIND

I'd hate to figure what walk-outs have cost this country!

DANIEL

Yes. I often wonder why it wouldn't be cheaper to
keep the men contented.

GOODKIND

How're you going to do it? Don't forget there are
as many people paid for stirring up strikes as for
crushing 'em! Paid well, too! What the laboring man
needs is a real interest in his job!

DANIEL

Why don't you give it to him?

GOODKIND

How? By doubling his wages? The more most of
'em get the less they want to do for it! You know
that!

DANIEL

Yes.

GOODKIND

They've got a notion that you get rich by riding around in a limousine!

DANIEL

Don't you?

GOODKIND

Not often! Not unless you think while you ride . . . or your father thought for you! Even then, money doesn't stay long in bad company! To hear those fellows you'd think there *wasn't* any work, except what's done with a pick! The man that really produces is the man with the idea!

DANIEL

The man that produces most.

GOODKIND

Yes, and he ought to *get* most!

DANIEL

He does!

GOODKIND

He always will! Show me a big man and I'll show you somebody who's done a big job! It's the little man with no capacity and no chin that cries about a conspiracy to keep him from being President!

DANIEL

There've got to be little men, too, Mr. Goodkind.

Goodkind

And they've got to be satisfied with little rewards! We can't all have the same bank-roll any more than we can all have the same health! That's where unions go wrong! When you tell a man he's going to have the same reward, whatever he does—not because he's got ability, but because he's got a union card—down goes the standard, out goes incentive, and to hell goes the whole social structure!

Daniel

Right!

Goodkind

That's why I'm fighting the unions! Not because I want to starve the man who works, but because I want to fire the man who doesn't . . . *and* reward the man who does! I want to give every man a good reason for doing his best! You can talk equality and democracy all you like, Dan, but the minute the average man isn't afraid of being fired he isn't afraid of being worthless! The minute you take away incentive—the chance to get *this*—that minute you reduce the world to a common level of common indifference and common futility!

Daniel

Right!

Goodkind

[*Rising*]: Have another cigar! [Daniel *shows the one he has just lighted, and shakes his head.*] Where the hell's——[*He turns, and sees* Benfield *standing in the door L.*] Oh, Benfield! Come in! Gilchrist has settled the strike!

BENFIELD

Good!

DANIEL

[*Giving a folded document to* GOODKIND]: There are the terms. [GOODKIND *sits L.*] They may seem a little radical, but I think I can show you they'll save money in the end!

GOODKIND

That's the idea!

[*With the paper in his hands, being opened, he feels confident and cocky. To* BENFIELD]: I told you I knew my man! The Lord knows he's full of theories, but sometimes they—[*His eye falls upon a disturbing line*] Wait a minute! What's this?

BENFIELD

What's what?

GOODKIND

[*Reading*]: "Hereby agreed . . . the men are to be represented . . . on the board of directors. . . ."

BENFIELD

[*Stunned*]: No!!

GOODKIND

Yes! And . . . look here! [*Reading*] "All disputes . . . referred . . . to a committee of arbitration . . ."

BENFIELD

The man's gone crazy!

DANIEL

When you're through . . .

GOODKIND

[*Reading*]: "One-half of all profits, over and above a fair dividend, to be divided pro rata, according to wage and length of service." [*He rises*] Why . . . [*Words fail*] What is this?

BENFIELD

Jerry told you; it's surrender!

DANIEL

No! No! It's justice!

GOODKIND

It's nothing! It's a scrap of paper until I sign it, and I wouldn't sign it if I had to shut up every mine in West Virginia! Why should I? We've got 'em licked!

DANIEL

If you'll only let me explain . . .

GOODKIND

Explain *what?* They're licked! They sent a delegation up here, and we've won over the delegation!

DANIEL

You mean you've *bought* the delegation!

GOODKIND

Who said so?

DANIEL

Jerry. . . . Not ten minutes ago he referred to Stedtman as the company detective. We both know Hennig's for sale. Buy him, and I'll go back and tell them he's bought, and prove it!

BENFIELD

You're working for us!

DANIEL

I'm working for——

GOODKIND

Wait a minute, Benfield! We've all lost our heads! Daniel and I have just been over all this, and he admitted I was right!

DANIEL

Right as far as you went, but you only went part way! You have a right to a profit on your idea, and your investment, and the labor you put back of it! The public has a right to coal, and transportation, and all it needs and pays for! But, above everything else, the workman who works honestly has a right to something more than the barest kind of a bare living . . . and it can all be done if you don't sink everybody's rights to accumulate a fortune you don't need and can't use! . . . All the argument on earth can't make you *all* right so long as there's a Umanski in the World!

GOODKIND

If these people succeed there's no limit to what they'll do!

DANIEL

If they fail there's no limit to what you'll do!

GOODKIND

There's no good transferring control from the intelligent few to the ignorant mob!

DANIEL

There's no good in anything so long as we fight each other like beasts, instead of helping each other like brothers! There's no hope anywhere except in The Great Teacher, and the understanding that what He taught was not only good morals, but good sense and good business!

BENFIELD

Highfalutin nonsense!

GOODKIND

Daniel doesn't realize what he's costing us!

DANIEL

What?

GOODKIND

Millions!

DANIEL

Oh, is that all?

BENFIELD

All?

DANIEL

Am I costing you one cigar? Am I costing you one blanket from your warm beds, or one stick of furniture from your comfortable homes, or anything else you'll ever miss? I'm taking nothing from you, and I'm giving thousands of men like you a chance to live!

GOODKIND

You're costing yourself your last chance of success!

DANIEL

I don't want your kind of success! I'm through! I give you back your job, as I gave you back your church, and I give you twenty-four hours to sign that paper!

GOODKIND

If I do, you're finished!

DANIEL

I am when you've signed! [*He goes R.*]

GOODKIND

If you walk out of that door you're throwing away the chance of your life!

DANIEL

I'm keeping my soul! [*He opens the door.*]

BENFIELD

You Judas!

GOODKIND

You damned fool!

DANIEL

Good-night!
[DANIEL *closes the door behind him.*]

THE CURTAIN FALLS.

ACT III.

SCENE: "Overcoat Hall." New York.

*This room—not too large—was the "front parlor"
of a comfortable residence in down-town New York.
Business, of the least attractive sort, and the slums
long since have occupied the district. The building is
a red-brick, low-stoop, English-basement house. The
rear wall, which is the front of the dwelling, is pierced
by two lofty windows, through which are seen the top of
an iron railing, and a row of similar structures, fallen
into decay, across the street. Between these windows,
upon a low marble shelf, now holding a tray of cups
and saucers, originally was a tall, gold-framed mirror.
Over this hangs a blackboard, upon which has been
chalked: "And so, to the end of history, hate shall
breed hate, murder shall breed murder, until the gods
create a race that can understand." Beneath the right
window is a big radiator. Down stage R. are folding
doors, partly open, or a large single door—whichever
shall prove advisable. These—or this—lead to the
main hall, and so to the basement, or upstairs, or to
the front door, which slams solidly whenever it is
closed. Left is a decrepit, white-marble mantel, with
a "fake" fireplace. In front of this—in a jog, perhaps—a small platform, of the kind used in public
schools. Upon this, a small table and a chair. Down*

109

*stage of it, a geographical globe, suspended over which
a wall-pad informing us that today is Wednesday.
Above the mantel-shelf, another blackboard, upon which
are some simple calculations, and the axiom, "Luck is
work." In the center of the room is a long library
table, with a brown cover, and with numerous kitchen
chairs about it. On the table a reading lamp, a bowl
of yellow, purple and brown chrysanthemums; and numerous books and magazines. Gilchrist has succeeded in
making the old place comfortable and inviting. It is
a combination of club, settlement house, school, reading
room and lecture hall. Brown linoleum covers the
floor, and there are brown denim curtains over the windows. A history chart hangs on the wall. There are
book-shelves, and two or three big, comfortable chairs;
a phonograph and, perhaps, even a motion picture machine.*

AT RISE: *It is just after seven o'clock on a brisk
evening in late October, 1920.*

*Grubby, seated down stage of the center table, is
concealed behind a copy of "The Woman's Home Companion," which he has opened wide, and holds in front
of him.*

*Mack, a shabby ne'er-do-well, between thirty and
forty years old, opens the doors R., and peers in uncertainly. Reassured by the character of the room, he
enters, and looks about him curiously. Even from the
rear, it is evident that Grubby is a person of no authority, so Mack dismisses him, temporarily, and warms his
hands over the radiator. Next he inspects the quo-*

*tation between the windows, pauses at the phonograph,
and arrives in front of the platform L. The three
words on this blackboard interest him. He reads them,
turns away, turns back, and reads them again. At
last, he sniffs contemptuously, and, completing his cir-
cuit, stops on the left of Grubby.*

MACK

Hello . . . you!

[GRUBBY *lowers his paper, and reveals a sixty-year-old
face, round, very red, and framed in a scraggly
gray beard.*]

Is this Overcoat Hall?

GRUBBY

Yes.

MACK

I'm looking for Mr. Gilchrist.

GRUBBY

He ain't in, but he will be.

MACK

Are you working here?

GRUBBY

No.

MACK

Is *anybody* working here?

GRUBBY

Mary Margaret.

MACK

Who's she?

GRUBBY

A girl.

MACK

What girl?

GRUBBY

The girl that cleans. A lame girl. Her mother's the janitor. Have a seat. Somebody'll be along in a minute.

[*And he resumes his magazine . . . never completely abandoned. Mack, thrown upon his own resources, picks up one periodical after another, but Fortune does not smile. They prove to be "The Atlantic Monthly" . . . "The Review of Reviews" . . . "The Scientific American."*]

MACK

What are you reading?

GRUBBY

A piece about "Better Babies."

MACK

[*Laughs*]: Are you going into the baby business?

GRUBBY

No. I was a hansom driver.

MACK

Handsome! [*The laugh becomes uproarious.*]

GRUBBY

Ah . . . hacks! I drove hacks . . . man and boy . . . forty years. Then taxis come in, and I went out!

Mack

What'd you do then?

Grubby

Took to drink.

Mack

Yeh; then drink went out.

Grubby

What's *your* job?

Mack

Well, I was in the movies. That is, I was going to be, but the fellow that was going to put up the money, his mother didn't die, after all. . . . Before that, I sold bricks . . . a few weeks. I sold books, too. And life insurance. I never had any luck. Who wrote that, "Luck is Work"?

Grubby

Mr. Gilchrist.

Mack

Well, it isn't! I've worked at *fifty* things, and look at me! I figure the world owes *me* a living, and here I am, waiting for a bite of grub and an overcoat! Is it true the boss'll give you an overcoat?

Grubby

He will if he's got one.

Mack

That's what a fellow told me. He said that's why they call this Overcoat Hall.

GRUBBY

Yes.

MACK

I suppose a hard-luck story's the proper spiel.

GRUBBY

You don't get no chance for a spiel. He don't ask you nothing. You just come, and help yourself, and talk things over . . . if you want to. Coffee and sandwiches every night—and suppers and sermons on Wednesdays.

MACK

Preaching! [*Looks at the wall pad, and reaches for his hat.*] Wednesday. I'll be back Thursday.

GRUBBY

Not regular preaching! Just talks! Sometimes they's a picture show . . . but the pictures is rotten! No shooting, or nothing! But you can always sneak a little snooze 'til you get to the hand-out!

[MARY MARGARET *enters through the open door R. Her two crutches are rubber-tipped, so her invasion is noiseless. She occupies herself with the cups and saucers C.* MARY MARGARET *is fifteen, and pathetically pretty. The conspicuous feature of her costume is a pair of soiled gold slippers that once set off a ball gown.*]

MACK

Don't he try to reform you?

GRUBBY

Naw! The way he talks, you'd think you was as good as him. He says to me, the other night, he says, "You're a good man yet, Grubby," he says. "You're strong and healthy," he says, "and, if you learned to drive a taxi, all the best people in New York would be telephoning for your cab. I'll lend you the money," he says. Gee; he almost had me started!

MACK

What's the catch?

GRUBBY

I don't know.

MACK

There must be graft in it somewhere.

GRUBBY

If you ask me, I think the poor gent's got a few nuts in his nose-bag. A little bit batty. That's what *I* say!

MARY MARGARET

[*Turning down*]: And that's what you got no right to say, Grubby!

GRUBBY

[*To* MACK]: Mary Margaret.

MARY MARGARET

He's been good to you, ain't he?

GRUBBY

That's why we think he's nutty. What's he do it for?

Mary Margaret

'Cause he loves you.

Grubby

What for?

Mary Margaret

God knows! [*She has brought down a cup and sau-
cer, with other utensils, and is clearing and setting a
place at one end of the table. With this exclamation,
she locates the cup somewhat forcibly.*] After seven
o'clock now, and the meeting in half an hour, and he
ain't had a bite since morning!

Mack

Where *is* he?

Mary Margaret

He went to see a man that killed himself. [Mack
laughs] I mean . . . tried to. It was in the papers
this afternoon, and Mr. Gilchrist says: "I want to
talk to that man." [Mack's *interposition has brought
his words to her mind, and reflecting on them, she ex-
plodes.*] Graft!! Why he didn't have the rent money
yesterday, and he was desprit! He ain't had money,
to get himself a pair of shoes, and nobody helps him,
or comes near him, but you bums that roast him behind his back! [Goodkind *appears in the doorway R.*]

Grubby

I didn't roast him. I just said he was crazy.

Goodkind

[*Crisply*]: Mr. Gilchrist?

MARY MARGARET

He'll be here any minute.   Won't you come in?

GOODKIND

Thanks.

[*He comes forward a few steps, and looks at* GRUBBY, *who, after an instant, takes refuge behind his Home Companion.* GOODKIND *crosses to* MACK, *who turns up stage.   He surveys the blackboard.* MARY MARGARET *finishes her task.*]

MARY MARGARET

[*Offering a periodical to* GOODKIND]: Take a magazine, and sit down.   [*With a nod, he accepts.*]   I got to go make the coffee.   [*To* GRUBBY] You can come and carry it up in about fifteen minutes.   [*She turns and catches* MACK *filching a loaf of sugar.*]   Graft!! . . . Well, you ought to know!   [*She exits R., singing "I'm a Pilgrim."   By now,* GOODKIND *is reading in a big chair L.* MACK *glances at him, and comes down to* GRUBBY.]

MACK

Think she'll tell *him?*

GRUBBY

Naw!   Anyway, he don't care!   He says we're all brothers in God.

MACK

Gee!

GRUBBY

That's what he told Jimmie Curran—brothers in God—and Jimmie just up for pinchin' a guy's pants.

Jimmie lives across from his room upstairs, and Jimmie says he's clean loco. [GOODKIND *notes name and address on the margin of his magazine.*] Guess what he's got in the back yard!

MACK

What?

GRUBBY

Tennis. And handball games for children. And, in the other two houses, he's got flats . . . with bathtubs . . . and the rents ain't what they ask now for stalling a horse. Why wouldn't I say he was crazy? Everybody says so but Mary Margaret!

[DANIEL *enters R. He is shabby, but beaming. He carries two books, which he lays on some piece of furniture up R.; after which he removes his overcoat, and hangs it over an old umbrella already suspended from a wall-rack down stage of the door.*]

DANIEL

Hello, Grubby! You're early! And you've brought a friend! That's fine! [*He shakes hands with* MACK.] You're very welcome! [*Sees and crosses to* GOODKIND] And Mr. Goodkind! Well! You're welcome, too! [*Shakes hands*] Have you come down to look us over?

GOODKIND

[*His eyes indicating the others*]: I've come down on personal business.

DANIEL

Oh, yes! [*Turns*] Grubby, there's a box of books in the hall. How would you and your friend like to——

GRUBBY

I promised to help with the coffee.

DANIEL

I see. [GRUBBY *exits. To* MACK, *who has been stealing surreptitious glances at the overcoat*] And you?

MACK

I just wanted to speak to you a minute.

DANIEL

All right. After the meeting.

MACK

I wanted to ask you——

DANIEL

After the meeting! [*Turns back to* GOODKIND] Sit down.

GOODKIND

[*Sitting*]: Thanks.

[MACK—*resentful, unobserved, uncertain of getting the coat honestly—is sorely tempted. One pull, one step, and he is safe from work and denial. During the following, standing almost in the doorway, he is drawing the garment toward him.*]

DANIEL

[*To* GOODKIND]: I'm glad you dropped in tonight, because I've been intending to call on you, but there's

so much to do here—[*The coat comes off the rack, and
with it, the umbrella, which falls with a crash. Both
men rise, discovering* MACK, *coat in hand.*] Hello! I
thought you'd gone.

MACK

No; I—I—wanted——

DANIEL

You wanted my coat.

MACK

[*Advancing with a glad smile of pretended relief that*
DANIEL *has found the simple explanation*]: Yes . . .
that's what I wanted to ask you.

DANIEL

I'm so glad you said so. [MACK *shows surprise.*]
Because, if you hadn't and I hadn't understood, you
might have been tempted to take it without asking—
and then you'd've been so sorry and ashamed. A man
couldn't come into another man's house, and be wel-
comed, and then take the other man's coat, without
losing his self-respect . . . could he? And, of course,
if we're going to pull ourselves together, and get out
of a hole, we *must* keep our self-respect.

MACK

I wouldn't steal——

DANIEL

You couldn't. . . . It's your coat. . . . You asked
for it, and I gave it to you. . . . When you've worn it

. . . into a good job . . . come back and help me give
another to someone who needs it as you do.

MACK

I will.

DANIEL

Of course you will. [*Helps him into the coat, and
then shakes his hand.*] Good-night.

MACK

[*Hesitates, amazed*]: Good-night. [DANIEL *turns
L., and with a gesture expressive of the conviction that
this man is mad,* MACK *exits.*]

GOODKIND

Well, I'll be damned! [DANIEL *laughs*] He won't
come back! Not one in ten would come back!

DANIEL

All right! . . . That coat cost twenty dollars. If
one in ten *does* come back, we've made a man for two
hundred dollars. Isn't it worth the price?

GOODKIND

Maybe . . . if a man's *got* the price! Have you?

DANIEL

Like our friend . . . that's what I wanted to ask
you.

GOODKIND

It's not what I wanted to ask *you.*

DANIEL

I'm rather badly in need of money, and my father——

GOODKIND

Your father understood you well enough to leave you only an income. I foolishly turned over some of the principal, and, in three months, you threw away twenty thousand dollars. You could have had a big salary, and you threw *that* away. You're an utter damned waster—if you're no worse!

DANIEL

What do you mean . . . worse?

GOODKIND

You'll soon find out what I mean! You've had my son's wife down here, haven't you?

DANIEL

Once or twice.

GOODKIND

Or three times . . . or a dozen! *He* knows!

DANIEL

I've asked her not to come again.

GOODKIND

And *he's* asked her . . . but she's coming when she likes. She says so. Because she's in love with you. . . . God knows what women see in your kind of man! There was Pearl Hennig——

DANIEL

Please!

GOODKIND

Oh, my son told me! And I hear . . . in the neighborhood . . . that you've worse women than that running here! Women of the streets!

Daniel

Not many. They're welcome, but they don't come.

Goodkind

Well, that's *your* business! And if your neighbors get sick of having a resort of this kind in their midst, and drive you out, *that's* your business! But my son's wife——

Daniel

Is *her* business!

Goodkind

And *his!* Only Jerry's in no condition to settle the matter! He's broken down from worry and overwork, and you're partly responsible, and that puts it up to me! You can take this as a final warning! If you see Clare again, I'll act, and I'll act quick! That's all! Good-night! [*He gathers up his coat and hat, and crosses to the door.*]

Daniel

[*Waking from a reverie, and turning R.*] Oh! Mr. Goodkind!

Goodkind

[*Expecting capitulation. Comes down R.*]: Yes?

Daniel

How about the money?

Goodkind

You've had what's coming to **you!**

DANIEL

But that's *nothing!* I pay half that for these crazy houses! And I've gone terribly in debt fitting them up!

GOODKIND

With bath tubs and tennis courts!

DANIEL

People must have baths.

GOODKIND

These dirty immigrants!

DANIEL

The dirtier they are, the worse they need 'em. I want to show them how to live, and I want to show other people that you don't have to make a pigpen to make a profit!

GOODKIND

Are you making a profit?

DANIEL

Enormous! And, to go on, I've got to have twenty-two thousand dollars.

GOODKIND

Oh, is that all? Twenty-two thousand dollars to go on making a fool of yourself! Well, you won't get it!

DANIEL

Not even as an advance?

GOODKIND

Not a penny!

DANIEL

Don't drive me to——

GOODKIND

To what?

DANIEL

[*Rather at a loss*]: To ask for an accounting!

GOODKIND

[*Hardly believing his own ears*]: To ask for . . . WHAT? [*This is the last straw.*] Now listen to me! I've stood all I'm going to stand! You've run amuck! You've become dangerous to yourself . . . and me . . . and the neighborhood! You're going to stop it, and you're going to stop now!

DANIEL

That's your mistake.

GOODKIND

Is it? A year ago you gave me twenty-four hours to sign a paper, and I did it, and it cost me two million dollars! Tonight I give you thirty minutes to shut up this place, and quit seeing my daughter, and if you don't do it——

DANIEL

As I won't!

GOODKIND

I'll be here inside of half an hour with a doctor!

DANIEL

And then?

GOODKIND

Then we'll file a petition to have you declared **incompetent**! [*He starts R.*]

DANIEL

Mr. Goodkind, you don't mean that! You don't mean that because I'm trying to help——

GOODKIND

Help . . . whom? Strikers, and street women, and general riff-raff! And you don't even help *them* . . . because nobody *can*! And, if you *could*, and *did*, how in the name of God would that help the Community? If I find you're still crazy in half an hour, I'll *say* you're crazy, and *I'll prove it*! [*He goes to the door.*] Think it over! [*As he is about to exit, he narrowly escapes collision with a neatly-dressed, capable-looking man, who apologizes, in nearly correct English, and, with a contemptuous glance, crosses to up C.*]

THE MAN

Excuse me!

GOODKIND

All right! [*He follows the man back into the room.*] Haven't I seen you somewhere before?

THE MAN

Yes, sir. My name's Umanski.

GOODKIND

Umanski? [*He remembers*] You're not the Pole who came to my house last year with a delegation?

UMANSKI

Yes.

GOODKIND

Well, I'll be——[DANIEL *fills his pipe from a jar on the mantelpiece L.*]

UMANSKI

Mr. Gilchrist tell me stay in New York. He's teach me English, and find me good job. I'm work now eight hours on the docks, and six on myself. [GOODKIND *again starts to go.*]

DANIEL

Mr. Goodkind! [GOODKIND *turns*] Umanski's got an invention. If you'll see it——

GOODKIND

I'll see *you* in . . . half an hour! [*He exits.*]

UMANSKI

What's *he* doing down here, Mr. Gilchrist?

DANIEL

He says I'm crazy, and he's going to shut up this place. Of course, he won't. [*He opens a book.*]

UMANSKI

Don't be too sure.

DANIEL

Nonsense! [*He sits*] I made him angry. [*He marks a passage.*] And somebody's told him a lot of lies!

UMANSKI

Somebody's told a good many people lies! Yesterday I heard a man say you run this house to . . . to . . . [*He hesitates.* DAN *looks up.*] . . . to get women!

DANIEL

Who said that?

UMANSKI

A wop named Malduca.

DANIEL

Oh, yes! I took his daughter in here once . . . for a week . . . until he got sober.

UMANSKI

They's a good many like that.

DANIEL

Oh, not a good many!

UMANSKI

Enough to make trouble. Why not you carry a pistol?

DANIEL

It's generally men with pistols that get shot.

UMANSKI

One of them fellows get you———[*Enter* MARY MARGARET.]

DANIEL

[*Warning him*]: Sh!

MARY MARGARET

I s'pose you ain't had any supper.

DANIEL

Not yet. [GRUBBY *enters with a tray, from which* MARY MARGARET *transfers dishes to the table.*]

UMANSKI

I brought you some money.

DANIEL

Money?

UMANSKI

My boss he give me another raise. He gonna make *me* boss after while. So I like to begin pay back what you lend me. [*Takes out bills.*]

DANIEL

Wait 'til you've sent for your family.

UMANSKI

I'm gonna send now. My big boy I'm gonna send school . . . college, maybe. That pump I make she goes fine. I show my boss . . . like you say . . . because he know about coal mines . . . and he say if she work she save whole lots of lives and money. She work, all right! [*He has put down the bills, and brought forth an English grammar.*] How about I go upstairs and study?

DANIEL

Sure! Go right up to my room! I'll be along after the meeting! [UMANSKI *exits*. GRUBBY *starts to follow*.] Where are you going, Grubby?

GRUBBY

Sandwiches! [*He exits*.]

MARY MARGARET

[*Down L.*]: Your supper's ready!

DANIEL

Thanks. [*Looks up*] What's this we're wearing? Golden slippers?

MARY MARGARET

Uh-huh! I took 'em out of the barrel of clothes that pretty lady sent.

DANIEL

[*Sitting at table*]: Supper with Cinderella!

MARY MARGARET

[*Setting dish before him*]: Gee, I love that story! [*She sits beside him, facing front*.] When you tell it to me, you make me believe I'm her.

DANIEL

If you believe it . . . you *are*.

MARY MARGARET

I guess believin' ain't never goin' to make *me* dance.

DANIEL

You can't tell . . . if you believe hard enough.

MARY MARGARET

That's what you said before, and I've tried, but, somehow, it don't work.

DANIEL

That's the very time to go on. If we stop, just because it don't work, that isn't faith.

MARY MARGARET

No; I s'pose not.

DANIEL

And faith moves mountains. Once upon a time there was a woman who'd been sick twelve years.

MARY MARGARET

What was the matter with her?

DANIEL

I don't know. But there was a Man in that city who said He could even make the dead rise. And everybody laughed at Him . . . as they would today. But the woman didn't laugh, and one morning, when He was passing her house, she got up and followed Him . . . just to touch the hem of His cloak. And what do you think?

MARY MARGARET

I duno.

DANIEL

She was cured. And the Man said——

MARY MARGARET

Oh, now, I know. "Thy faith hath made thee whole."

DANIEL

That's right.

MARY MARGARET

Could God do that for me?

DANIEL

Why not?

MARY MARGARET

It would be an awful big favor.

DANIEL

But if He doesn't, you must go on. If faith doesn't heal our hurts, it helps us to bear them. And that's almost the same thing, isn't it?

MARY MARGARET

[*Doubtfully*]: Yes.

DANIEL

Like believing you're Cinderella.

MARY MARGARET

Yes.

DANIEL

We can't decide what we want, and then be angry and doubtful because it doesn't happen our way. Because, all the time it's happening His way. The only thing we can be sure of is that He knows what's best.

MARY MARGARET

That's right. . . . You mean, if God wants me to be well, some day He'll make me well?

DANIEL

If you believe hard enough.

MARY MARGARET

And if He don't?

DANIEL

Then *that's* right . . . if you believe hard enough.

MARY MARGARET

I will, Mr. Gilchrist. [*She rises*] You ain't touched
your supper.

DANIEL

I've had plenty.

MARY MARGARET

I'll send Grubby up for the tray.

[*She exits. DANIEL finishes, and puts up his napkin.
He observes that the window-shades have not been
drawn. Attends to that R. Facing L., with his
hand on the shade of the window L., he pauses to
look out. PEARL HENNIG enters. Pearl is 25,
and her clothes are cheaply flashy. An experi-
enced eye should lose no time in appraising her.
She has an air of alarm. She looks around for
DAN, and then isn't quite sure of him in the
shadows up stage.*]

PEARL

[*Uncertainly*]: Mr. Gilchrist? [*He half turns*]
Don't stand by that window!

DANIEL

Hello, Pearl! [*He draws the shade*] How well you're looking. [*Comes down*] What's the matter with the window?

PEARL

It ain't safe.

DANIEL

[*Smiling*]: Are *you* going to advise me to carry a pistol?

PEARL

No. Just to keep out o' sight of people that do.

DANIEL

Meaning?

PEARL

Meaning Joe Hennig.

DANIEL

I thought Joe was in Black River.

PEARL

He ain't. I told you he was ashamed to go home. I told you he was gonna stay here an' get you!

DANIEL

[*Sits on bench in front of table*]: Well?

PEARL

[*Down stage R. of table*]: Well . . . he stayed. I went to him . . . like I told you . . . an' said it wasn't you . . . an' ast him to take me back. An' he said I was a liar an' he was gonna get you. I told you all that!

DANIEL

Yes; I guess you did.

PEARL

While he was workin' up town I didn't hear nothin' about him. But a little while ago he lost his job, an' began hangin' around down here. An' he's been drinkin', an' talkin' wild, an' I come in to tell you.

DANIEL

That's kind of you, Pearl, but I'm not afraid of Joe.

PEARL

I am. . . . He's got his gang. . . . I *know*.

DANIEL

How do you know?

PEARL

[*Hesitates*]: Well, last night I met up with one of his pals. . . . An' *he'd* been drinkin'. An' he said Joe said you was livin' on women, an' this place was a blind, an' nobody's wife was safe while you was in the neighborhood. An' this man said they was gonna get together, an' drive you out. They're dang'rous, Mr. Gilchrist. For God's sake, believe me! For God's sake, telephone the police!

DANIEL

There's no telephone here, Pearl. But there's always an officer at hand, and I'm among friends. Don't worry. Sit down, and wait for the meeting. I haven't seen you in ages.

PEARL

[*Doesn't sit. She is restless*]: Two weeks.

DANIEL

What are you doing?

PEARL

I'm workin' at Macy's.

DANIEL

Like it?

PEARL

[*Defiantly*]: Better than bein' with Joe.

DANIEL

If you'd stayed with Joe, maybe he wouldn't *be* drinking.

PEARL

He always did. That's why I ast you to stick around in Black River. That's one reason I quit.

DANIEL

One reason.

PEARL

[*Admitting it grudgingly*]: They was others. . . . I wanted good clothes, an' a good time . . . jus' like other women.

DANIEL

[*Thinking of* CLARE]: Yes . . . like other women.

PEARL

[*Indicating her costume*]: An' I've got 'em!

Daniel

Yes; you've "got 'em." But don't you think . . . sometimes . . . you and the other women . . . that they cost you too much?

Pearl

I don't get you.

Daniel

I only mean isn't there something worth more than good clothes and a good time? A good home, maybe, with love in it . . . and little children.

[Pearl *hesitates, and then the uneasiness she has never lost takes her up to peep out of the curtain.*]

Pearl

We oughtn't to be here talkin'.

Daniel

Why not?

Pearl

I'm frightened of Joe.

Daniel

You needn't be.

Pearl

I am. I can't help it. I got a hunch. I ain't told you all this man said, an' I ain't told you how he come to say it, but he said it was gonna be soon, an' I got a hunch sumpin's gonna happen *tonight*. Please let me go out an' phone! Please let me get the police! [Dan-

IEL *laughs*] You're crazy, Mr. Gilchrist! You're just crazy! [*An infinitesimal pause. She turns.*] An' I'm goin'! [*She runs to the door, which opens before her, and admits* CLARE GOODKIND. CLARE *is smartly gowned, in street attire, but somehow, she has the appearance of being disheveled . . . of having dressed in haste.*]

DANIEL

Clare—Mrs. Goodkind! [*A pause*] Mrs. Hennig's just going.

CLARE

Mrs. Hennig?

DANIEL

Pearl Hennig. You've heard your husband **mention** her name.

PEARL

I know your husband.

CLARE

I know you do. [*Her tone tells how much she knows.*]

PEARL

[*Quails*]: I guess you ain't got much use **for me.**

CLARE

Why? What's the difference between us?

PEARL

[*Unable to make it out*]: Well . . . good-night! [*She exits.*]

DANIEL

Clare, I asked you. . . .

CLARE

I'd nowhere else to go. I've left him.

DANIEL

Left . . . Jerry?

CLARE

Yes. For good. He struck me.

DANIEL

No!!

CLARE

Here . . . in the breast! And he's lying now . . . brandy-soaked and half-conscious . . . across the foot of my bed!

DANIEL

I can't . . . believe. . . .

CLARE

He's been drinking . . . more and more! And, of course, there've been women . . . from the beginning! All kinds of women! *That* woman, salesgirls, stenographers, women of our own class! Do you remember . . . in your church . . . a Mrs. Thornbury? He's been quite open about *her*! Tonight we were going out to dinner! He came to my room . . . drunk . . . and babbled that he'd refused to go until she was invited! Then *I* refused to go, and he accused me . . . *of you* . . . and struck me with his fist!

DANIEL

He accused . . . *you?*

CLARE

Yes. And then he tried to take me in his arms!
Night after night he's come to me . . . drunk . . .
and held me in his arms. And I said once there was
nothing more degrading than poverty! In the past two
years I've learned what degradation means! I've come
to see your way at last! I've come to realize that the
material things are nothing, and that love is all! It
isn't too late?

DANIEL

It's never too late!

CLARE

I knew you'd say that! I'll share your work . . .
your want . . . if need be . . . gladly! Only take me
away!

DANIEL

[*Not yet comprehending*]: But my work is here!

CLARE

We can't stay here! Jerry suspects us! He's made
his father suspect us! Do you know what they're plan-
ning to do now? [*He nods*] Jerry wants to send you
to an asylum! He said so tonight! And he'll do it,
too! The strange thing about Jerry is that, with his
mind going, and his health gone, he still gets what he
wants! Take me away, and "we'll have five or six
rooms, and each other!"

DANIEL

Clare!

CLARE

Don't you understand that I'm offering myself to you?

DANIEL

Yes; I understand!

CLARE

I love you! I need you! I've always loved you, and needed you, even when I lied to you, and myself! This is our last chance for happiness! I've been blind, and stupid, and cruel, but it isn't too late! Take me, and hold me, and we'll both forget!

DANIEL

Forget?

CLARE

Forget everything! Won't you take me, dear?

DANIEL

No!

CLARE

Don't you want me?

DANIEL

No!

CLARE

That's not true! You love me! You've always loved me! Look at me, and deny it if you can!

DANIEL

I don't deny it! I love you!

CLARE

Then take me!

DANIEL

I love the good in you . . . the good you're trying so hard to kill! I love you because you're big enough to do what's right!

CLARE

What *is* right?

DANIEL

Go back to your husband!

CLARE

I'd rather die!

DANIEL

I'd rather you died . . . than *this!*

CLARE

Oh, you fanatic! You blind fanatic!

DANIEL

I love you!

CLARE

Love! You don't know what love means! You're only half a man!

DANIEL

And I'm praying to God, with all my strength, to save us from the other half!

CLARE

For what?

DANIEL

For you . . . and HIM . . . and for MY PEOPLE. [*Off R., very softly, as she goes down the hall,* MARY MARGARET *is heard singing "I'm a Pilgrim; I'm a Stranger."*] For the little girl out there.

CLARE

And for them you'd send me back to degradation?

DANIEL

That little girl's known degradation that you and I will never know. And she's singing. Her constant companions are poverty and pain. And she's singing. She's crippled. She may never walk again. And still she can say God's will be done. She believes in me. I can't disappoint her and the rest. I'm going on with my job, and you're going back to yours!

CLARE

You mean to Jerry?

DANIEL

Yes.

CLARE

You think *that's* God's will?

DANIEL

I know it's your job. You took it with your eyes open. It's up to you to see it through.

CLARE

Must I go on forever paying for one mistake?

DANIEL

Somebody must pay for our mistakes. That it was wrong to make a bargain doesn't make it right to break the bargain when we get tired of it.

CLARE

I don't know what to do.

DANIEL

Play the game. Go back to that poor, mistaken man lying across the foot of your bed—his mind going and his health gone. Bear your punishment and help him to bear his. That's your duty!

CLARE

Duty! Duty!! What about happiness?

DANIEL

There *is* no other happiness. Oh, don't you see, my dear, *that's* been your *great* mistake? You're always crying—you and the world—"I want to be happy!" Happiness is service! Happiness is clean-living, and clear-thinking, and self-forgetfulness, and self-respect!

CLARE

And love?

DANIEL

Love *isn't* all. Not the love you mean. You said: "Take me, and we'll both forget." Could we have forgotten promises unkept, faith disappointed, aspirations unrealized? No, my dear, love isn't all; nor even happiness. There's something bigger, and better, and more important, and that something is . . . DUTY!

CLARE

The world doesn't think that!

DANIEL

That's what's wrong with the world! [*A pause.*]

CLARE

You want me to go back?

DANIEL

I want you to be right!

CLARE

Well, then . . . I'm going through. I'm going back, and play the game . . . with you in my heart always. You don't forbid that, do you?

DANIEL

You are in mine always.

CLARE

And this isn't good-bye. Sometime . . . somewhere . . . in this world . . . or out of it . . . there must be a moment . . . and a place . . . to retrieve mistakes. . . . Good-night.
[*She starts up. He passes her, and opens the door.*]

DANIEL

Clare . . . good-night. [*She takes his hand. Then she exits. The outer door slams. Then a cab door*

... *faintly.* *He sinks* ... *tired with the effort of* *renunciation.* *Afterward he comes down, slowly, and* *drops on the bench in front of the table.* MARY MAR-GARET *enters, singing "I'm a Pilgrim," in a higher key,* *to march tempo, keeping time with her crutches.* *She* *is down R. when she sees* DANIEL.]

MARY MARGARET

Ain't you well, Mr. Gilchrist?

DANIEL

Just tired.

MARY MARGARET

Maybe you ain't believin' hard enough. [*He looks* *up.*] It's 'most time for the meetin'. [GRUBBY *enters* *with a tray.*]

GRUBBY

I brung the sandwiches.

[MRS. MULLIGAN *enters.* *She is the worse for liquor,* *and glad of a warm place to enjoy it.* *She slinks* *in rather furtively, and sits R. end of table.* *She* *is followed on by* MR. *and* MRS. HENCHLEY. *He* *is a middle-aged and respectable locksmith.* *She* *is larger than he, and somewhat formidable.*]

MARY MARGARET

Good evening, Mrs. Mulligan.

MRS. MULLIGAN

[*With a hiccough*]: It is not!

GRUBBY

[*Aside to* MARY MARGARET]: Bums . . . like that
. . . ain't got no business here.

MR. HENCHLEY

Good evening, Mary Margaret. [*She nods.*]

MRS. HENCHLEY

Good evening, Mr. Gilchrist.

DANIEL

Good evening, and welcome.

MR. HENCHLEY

[*To* DANIEL]: I guess we're early.

MRS. HENCHLEY

[*To* DANIEL]: Yes. I wanted to speak to you . . .
about Mr. Henchley's pants.

DANIEL

Mr. Henchley's *what?*

MRS. HENCHLEY

Pants. I took out a spot . . . with gasoline . . .
and hung 'em on the fire-escape that runs across from
this house, and to-night they was gone, and I think you
ought to look into your lodgers.

DANIEL

I will.
[*Enter* MISS LEVINSON. *She is a Jewess—a garment-
worker; thoughtful, studious, spectacled.*]

MISS LEVINSON

Good evening, everybody!

DANIEL

Good evening, Miss Levinson.
[*The others, too, acknowledge the greeting.*]

MISS LEVINSON

I've brought back your book.

MRS. HENCHLEY

What've you been reading?

MISS LEVINSON

George Bernard Shaw.

MRS. HENCHLEY

I s'pose you ain't read "The Sheik"?

MISS LEVINSON

[*With justifiable pride*]: I've been reading "Cæsar and Cleopatra."

DANIEL

[*Taking the volume*]: That's where we got the quotation on the board. I've jumbled it a bit. [*Reads*] "And so, to the end of history, hate shall breed hate, murder shall breed murder, until the gods create a race that can understand."

MISS LEVINSON

That's it; isn't it? A race that can—
[*The door is opened violently, and enter* PEARL HENNIG.]

PEARL

Mr. Gilchrist!

DANIEL

Oh, Pearl; I thought you'd gone.

PEARL

No; I've been watchin', an' I've got to speak to you
. . . *quick!*

DANIEL

In just a few minutes.

PEARL

Now! Joe's out there!

MRS. MULLIGAN

Ah, shut up!

DANIEL

Mrs. Mulligan! . . . Pearl; you're interrupting!
. . . You were saying, Miss Levinson?

MISS LEVINSON

We seem always to have hated everything different
from ourselves . . . in station, or race, or religion.

DANIEL

Yes. It's stupid . . . and instinctive. I've noticed
we're inclined to blame a man for a pug nose . . . if
ours is Roman. Some day we'll get over the idea that
all who differ from us are villains, and that we should
hate each other instead of trying to understand each

other. It was on the battlefields that I came to believe a man's life might well be given to teaching and to preaching . . . love! [*A solid half-brick crashes through a practical pane of glass in the window L. Everybody screams and rises.*] Don't be alarmed. It's only some hoodlum!

PEARL

Mr. Gilchrist . . . it's Joe! I seen him in front! That's why I couldn't get out! Somebody go get the police! [*A general movement.*]

DANIEL

No!

PEARL

He's got other men with him! He'll kill you! [*The front door slams. Pearl hurls herself against the door R.*] Here he comes! Don't let him in! Somebody help me hold this door! [*In spite of her, the door slowly opens.*]

DANIEL

Pearl! Stand aside! [*Enter* GOODKIND.] It's only Mr. Goodkind!

GOODKIND

Yes. And your neighbors are calling.

MR. HENCHLEY

What's the matter?

MRS. HENCHLEY

Is there any danger?

}Together

MARY MARGARET

I'll get the cops.

Voices in the Gang

[*Off stage*]: The fake! The damned pimp! Drive him out! Come on. . . . Rush him!

[*Suddenly there is the noise of the oncoming.* Pearl *throws herself before* Dan. Mary Margaret *is just behind him. The others retreat to the platform. Headed by* Joe Hennig . . . *drunk* . . . *the rowdies enter—*Jimmie Curran, *a big dockman, his wife and half a dozen hangers-on of the neighborhood.*]

Joe

[*En route*] Come on, fellows! We'll show this guy! We'll show— [*He confronts them*] By God! Caught in the act! [*To his gang*] That's my wife!

Daniel

Caught in what act, Joe?

Joe

Why . . . caught . . . in the act. . . .

Daniel

Tell him what we're here for. . . . You, Grubby.

Grubby

[*Following the example of* Peter]: I don' want to get in no trouble!

Mary Margaret

I'll tell you.

Daniel

No, Mary Margaret!

Umanski

[*Who has come through the crowd unobserved; claps his hand on* Joe's *shoulder, forcing him to his knees*]: I tell you!

Joe

Umanski!

Umanski

I tell you, Hennig! Mr. Gilchrist been friend to everybody! And now, when *he* need friend, nobody knows nothing! Well, *I* know! I know anybody hurt him gotta lick me!

Daniel

No . . . please . . . Umanski!

Joe

Lickin' people ain't gonna hide facks!

Umanski

[*Threatening with his free fist*]: Shall I?

Daniel

No . . . no!

[Umanski *sets* Joe *on his feet.* Joe *turns eloquently to his gang.*]

Joe

I'll show you the kind of fake that's been foolin' you! He was a preacher, an' he got kicked out of his church!

VOICES IN THE GANG

Kicked out! They got onto you, did they? Caught him with the goods!

JOE

He was a spy for the people that live on labor, and he came to the mines, where we was on strike, and ran away with my wife!

VOICES IN THE GANG

The dirty bum! Maybe he didn't get much!

PEARL

It *wasn't* him!

JOE

She says that 'cause she's stuck on him!

PEARL

I ain't!

JOE

Well, you're workin' for him, ain't you?

PEARL

No!

DANIEL

Your wife's working in a store uptown!

VOICES IN THE GANG

We know different! What's she doing here? That's a good one! What're you giving us? Everybody in the neighborhood knows what she's doing!

JOE

My wife's walking the streets!

DANIEL

That's a lie!

JOE

I heard from a pal she picked up las' night . . . an'
I *seen* her comin' here!

JIMMIE

She's workin' Sixth Avenue!

MRS. MULLIGAN

I can't believe it! I can't believe it!

DANIEL

Pearl!!! . . . It *is* a lie?

PEARL

Oh, no! . . . It's true. [*A momentary silence; the
gang jeers; she turns on them; then a momentary de-
fiance.*] Well! Well, why wouldn't it be? I tried to
live straight . . . like you told me . . . an' I *had* a
job . . . but when the other girls got wise. . . . They
ain't no better than I am! [*She slowly gives way before his calm, steady gaze.*] Anyway . . . I lied. I
am walkin' the streets. I ain't no good. I ain't fit to
live. [*She starts to sink at his feet. He raises her.*]

DANIEL

Pearl!

PEARL

For Christ's sake, ain't you done with me now?

DANIEL

For Christ's sake . . . no! [*And he takes her in his arms.*]

JOE

It's all fake! Ain't you fellows on? He's got every rotten woman in the neighborhood workin' for him. Your wives ain't safe! Your kids ain't safe! Ask Jimmie Curran! He knows what's goin' on here! [*Enter* TONY MALDUCA.] Ask Tony Malduca!

A VOICE

Here's Tony!

TONY

Why you send for me? What do you want?

JOE

We want to know what happened to your kid! Did he bring her in here . . . an' keep her . . . against her will? Did he?

TONY

That's what he done!

VOICES IN THE GANG

You remember Teresa Malduca? You see! Sure; everybody knows that! She was here a week!

UMANSKI

You damned wop!

DANIEL

Umanski!

VOICES IN THE GANG

There ain't no woman safe! He's a damned fake! Beat him up! Kill him!

JOE

That's it! Don't let this big guy buffalo you! Come on! Drive him out! [*To* DANIEL] I said I'd get you, an' I have! [*The gang presses closer, but* UMANSKI'S *menacing bulk still holds them off.*]

MARY MARGARET

[*Kneeling on the platform L.*]: Oh, dear God, please listen! [*And she begins the Lord's Prayer.*]

PEARL

Get the police!

MISS LEVINSON

[*Crying out of the window L.*]: Police! Police!

JIMMIE

[*To* UMANSKI]: Get out of the way . . . you!

A VOICE

Bust him in the jaw!

GOODKIND

[*Forcing his way through*]: Listen to me! No violence! You're dealing with a lunatic! Leave him alone! I've got a doctor coming in a few minutes! Leave him to me, and I give you my word I'll have this place closed tonight!

Voices in the Gang

Yes, and he'll open another one! Sure he will! Of course he will! Ah-h-h! Beat him up!

Goodkind

Leave him alone! You can't beat a crazy man!

Pearl

Mr. Gilchrist ain't crazy! He ain't a man! Ain't you seen what he just done to me?

A Woman

Hire a hall! [*All laugh.*]

Pearl

Ain't you heard? I lied to him, an' he's give me another chance, an' *I'm gonna take it!* He ain't no man! He's a Saint! I tell you he's like God!

A Voice

Where's his wings? [*All laugh.*]

Joe

Like God!

Jimmie

That's blasphemy!

Joe

That's what it is, an' that's what he's been tellin' 'em! Ain't it . . . you . . . Grubby? Didn't he tell you that, Jimmie? Didn't he tell you he was a Son of God?

VOICES IN THE GANG

Sure he did! That's right!

JOE

You see, that's what he's told 'em all! That's how
he gets 'em! [*To* DANIEL]: Didn't you tell 'em you
was a Son of God? [*There is a momentary silence,
broken only by* MARY MARGARET'S *prayer.*]

DANIEL

I am!

VOICES IN THE GANG

He admits it! And I'm Mary Magdalene! Pipe
Mary Magdalene! Son of God!

DANIEL

And so are we all! [*Jeers*] In you . . . and me
. . . and all of us . . . deep down . . . is something
of Him! We may try to hide it— [*Jeers*] —or kill
it, but, in spite of ourselves, we *are* Divine!

VOICES IN THE GANG

Chuck it! Hell! Cut the gab! He's crazy! Come
on; smash the place!

TONY

[*Facing* DANIEL]: If you're a Son of God . . .
save yourself! If you're . . . what you say . . . give
us a sign!

JOE

Ah, hell! Come on!

[*Two men have climbed upon the table, and suddenly
seize* UMANSKI *from behind. Momentarily, they*

bear him down, and this obstacle is removed. As
they drag him up R., the rest of the gang closes in
from all sides, hiding DANIEL, *who is forced up*
stage C. The table is overturned. Above the
struggling mass are seen fists striking down, va-
rious improvised weapons in action. A Dockman,
who, at JOE'S *speech, has lifted the bench from*
behind DANIEL, *to fell him with it, and whose*
weapon has been seized, from the rear, by the
HENCHLEYS, *pommels madly. Above the pande-*
monium are distinguished voices— PEARL: "*Help!*"
UMANSKI: "*I kill somebody!*"   MISS LEVINSON:
"*Police!*"   GOODKIND: "*Let him alone!*"   *Suddenly*
UMANSKI *throws off his captors, and, attacking*
the mob from in front, mows his way through,
tossing them to left and right. When a way is
cleared, he . . . and we . . . see DANIEL, *sense-*
less, lying in the overturned table, a tiny trickle
of blood running down his face, his head supported
by the table-leg R. UMANSKI *gives a deep groan*
of rage and pity. Hearing this and divining that
something dreadful has happened to her hero,
MARY MARGARET, *who has ceased praying, and*
raised herself to her feet by the aid of a neighbor-
ing chair, walks down to L. C. Before she sees
DANIEL, MISS LEVINSON *sees her, and emits a pierc-*
ing scream.]

MISS LEVINSON

Mary Margaret! Where are your crutches?

MARY MARGARET

[*Looking at her legs in tearful bewilderment*] I don't know! [*She tries them; then, in an hysterical cry*]: I kin walk! I kin walk! [*She looks for her benefactor . . . to show him.*] Mr. Gilchrist! Mr. Gilchrist! [*The crowd parts, and she sees the figure lying against the overturned table.*] Oh, Mr. Gilchrist! [*She folds him in her arms.*]

UMANSKI

[*Staring at* MARY MARGARET, *and in a tone of hushed awe*]: You wanted a sign—LOOK! Down on your knees—you murderers! God's in this room! Down on your knees!

[*One by one and two by two, the frightened mob obeys. JOE is lying senseless, but his cohorts, crossing themselves, have seen a miracle.*]

THE CURTAIN FALLS

ACT IV.

Scene: *Gilchrist's Room—"Upstairs."*
Two months later.

*The room is cheerful. That is its chief aspect.
Cheerful, and comfortable, and homelike. Such a room
. . . in the rear of the fourth story . . . might be had
anywhere for seven dollars a week, and its contents
duplicated for a couple of hundred, yet no one should
be able to look in without envying the occupant. Before the warm glow of a fireplace down R. is a big,
brown leather-covered armchair. An electric lamp
stands on a table stage left of the chair and squarely
opposite the fireplace. There are books on the table,
too, and writing things, and another chair on its left.
Above the grate a picture of Christ in the Temple.
Conspicuous in the flat, and visible from all parts of
the house, a big studio window. There are cream-
colored outside curtains, and brown denim inside curtains, drawn now, but when they are pulled aside, one
sees chimney-pots, and roof-tops, and a blue night-
sky, with one particularly bright star. Up L., a cur-
tained arch into a hall bedroom, and down L. a door.
The walls, covered with old-gold grass-cloth, are hid-
den, to a height of six feet, by roughly-built bookcases,
filled with much-used books. A sofa, against the wall*

161

L., now holds numerous packages. There is a brown-and-tan grass rug on the floor, and there may be a window seat, with brown cushions, beneath the window. The furniture is all old . . . probably second-hand . . . but, as aforesaid, the room suggests comfort and peace.

AT RISE: *It is just after eight o'clock, Christmas Eve, 1920.* DANIEL *is discovered, dreaming, in the armchair R., a pipe in his mouth and his face to the fire. He has not lighted the desk lamp, and, except for the glow of the embers, the room is in darkness. Hanging over the left arm of the chair,* DANIEL's *hand holds a magazine, but he has not begun reading. After a pause long enough for the audience to take in his surroundings, there is a light tap at the door and, without waiting for a response,* MARY MARGARET *enters. She walks without crutches—quite briskly—but plainly is on some secret business. Daniel is lost in the darkness. A package in her hand,* MARY MARGARET *crosses quickly to the table, and turns on one and then the other of the two lights in the lamp. Instantly, of course, she sees the figure in the chair, and conceals the package beneath her apron.*

MARY MARGARET

Mr. Gilchrist? [*He shows himself*] Goo'ness, how you scared me! I thought you went out!

DANIEL

No; I just slipped up here to read a while before we put our gifts on the tree. . . . Where's Grubby?

Mary Margaret

[*Contemptuously*]: Grubby!

Daniel

He promised to help with the packages.

Mary Margaret

Grubby's all swelled up with his new taxicab. Christmas Eve's the big night in his business, but he says don't worry . . . he'll be here in time for the sandwiches. Am I interruptin' your readin'?

Daniel

Oh, no! What have you there?

Mary Margaret

Where?

Daniel

Under your apron.

Mary Margaret

Oh!
[*She reveals the parcel*] I was gonna surprise you.
It's your Christmas present.

Daniel

From you?

Mary Margaret

[*Handing it across the table*]: Yes. It ain't much
. . . *you* know . . . an' I didn't want it on the tree

. . . before everybody. I wanted to give it to you my-self. Open it now. [*He does so. The package con-tains a framed picture.*]

DANIEL

Mary Margaret!

MARY MARGARET

The name's on the back! [*He turns it around, re-vealing to the audience a cheap and highly-colored chromo*] See . . . "Mama's Treasure."

DANIEL

It's just what I wanted.

MARY MARGARET

[*Delighted*]: Is it . . . honest? . . . Let's put it in place of that one over the mantel-piece! That's an awful pretty pitcher, but mine's got colors in it!

DANIEL

Why not in place of the Venus who fell on her nose?

MARY MARGARET

Oh, yes! [*She stands "Mama's Treasure" atop a bookcase L.*] It looks good, don't it?

DANIEL

Beautiful. I can't thank you enough. [*Takes her hand*] I can't really.

MARY MARGARET

You can't thank *me!* You that's give me— [*She looks down at her legs, and up again with eyes full of tears*] Oh, Mr. Gilchrist!

DANIEL

Now! Now! Now! We mustn't cry on Christmas!

MARY MARGARET

What're you going to do if you're happy?

DANIEL

Try laughing. [*She does*] Anyway, if I'm having my Christmas now, you must have yours. Suppose you rummage on the sofa.

MARY MARGARET

Oh! [*She runs to obey, and holds up a parcel inquiringly.*]

DANIEL

That's a book for Miss Levinson.

MARY MARGARET

[*Reads from another bundle*]: Mrs. Henchley. [*Takes up a third*] This one ain't marked.

DANIEL

Gloves for Mack. I wanted to show I appreciated his bringing back that coat.

MARY MARGARET

[*Reading from two packages*]: Peter . . . Paul . . .

DANIEL

For your brothers.

MARY MARGARET

[*With a fourth*]: And . . . Mary Margaret!

DANIEL

Open it now.

MARY MARGARET

[*Breathless, she comes to him C. Hesitates, and then, removing the wrapping, reveals a child's set in beaver—muff and neckpiece*]: Oh, Mr. Gilchrist! [*She tries them*] Oh, Mr. Gilchrist; you oughtn't! [*Looks about for a mirror*] They're beautiful! They're the most beautifulest furs I ever seen! I've wanted a set like this always! You've made me so happy! I never was so happy before in my life! [*And she begins to cry again.*]

DANIEL

Now! [*She remembers, and laughs.*]

MARY MARGARET

I don't know how to thank you.

DANIEL

Don't try.

MARY MARGARET

I never expected no such a Christmas! [*Starts for door*] I gotta show mother!

DANIEL

[*Turning R.*]: Take down a few of the packages!

Mary Margaret

I'll be back in a minute! [*She opens the door, disclosing* Goodkind. *Seriously alarmed*] Oh! . . . Mr. Gilchrist!

Daniel

[*Turning L.*]: Well . . . Mr. Goodkind!

Goodkind

May I come in?

Daniel

Of course! [*He enters. Dan indicates chair L. of table R.*] Sit down!

Goodkind

I've only a moment. Jerry's waiting for me in the car.

Daniel

How *is* Jerry? [Mary Margaret *arranges the chair.*]

Goodkind

[*Shakes his head despairingly. Looks at* Mary Margaret]: I wish you could perform a miracle on *him.*

Daniel

I wish I could.

Goodkind

[*To* Mary Margaret]: You seem to walk all right.

MARY MARGARET

Oh, yes!

GOODKIND

[*To* DAN]: Had a doctor look her over?

DANIEL

Three of 'em.

GOODKIND

Any opinion?

DANIEL

Three opinions.

MARY MARGARET

They said *he* didn't do it, and you seen him!

DANIEL

[*Holds up a warning finger*]: *Ssh!* [Then to GOODKIND] They all say she suffered from hysterical paraplegia. [GOODKIND *puzzled*] Hysterical paralysis. One says she was cured by shock—you know; the riot. Another says it was suggestion . . . believing . . . which is another way of saying faith, isn't it? The important thing is that she's cured!

MARY MARGARET

God did it—God and Mr. Gilchrist!

DANIEL

[*Hushing her again*]: Take down an armful of those packages . . . like a good girl!

MARY MARGARET

I will. [*She gathers them up, and, returning L. C., looks apprehensively at* GOODKIND] You call . . . if you want me! [*Exits*]

GOODKIND

[*Hesitates. Doesn't know how to begin. Takes cigars from his pocket*]: Smoke?

DANIEL

Thanks. [*Showing his pipe*] I'll stick to my old friend. [*He sits.*]

GOODKIND

How are things with you?

DANIEL

[*Enthusiastically*]: Fine!

GOODKIND

Happy?

DANIEL

[*Radiantly*]: Yes! . . . And you?

GOODKIND

No. Everything's . . . all wrong. My boy's very ill. Clare's wonderful to him. I can't explain it—she's like a different woman. And *she* seems happy. But Jerry's had to give up work, and there's more trouble in Black River, and that's what brought me!

DANIEL

You don't want *my* advice?

GOODKIND

I want *you* . . . as general manager. These strikes
are such utter damned waste! We had a working compromise on your agreement, and everything was all
right, but we began figuring we could make more money
. . . and the men walked out, and flooded the mines.
I'd like you to take charge, Daniel.

DANIEL

I can't.

GOODKIND

Name your own salary.

DANIEL

My work is here.

GOODKIND

You can have anything you want.

DANIEL

I don't want anything.

GOODKIND

You want to see the men get their rights.

DANIEL

They'll get 'em. Nothing can stop that.

GOODKIND

You're not going to turn down fifty thousand dollars
a year?

DANIEL

What can I buy with it that I haven't got?

GOODKIND

What can you buy with fifty——

DANIEL

What have *you* bought?

GOODKIND

I've got one of the finest houses in New York!

DANIEL

Is it any more comfortable than this?

GOODKIND

This one little room!

DANIEL

How many rooms do you live in at the same time?

GOODKIND

I've got half a dozen cars!

DANIEL

I've two legs, and I walk, and keep well.

GOODKIND

I've twenty servants——

DANIEL

Don't tell me you enjoy that!

GOODKIND

And the respect of people about me——

DANIEL

So have I!

GOODKIND

And, what's most important of all, I'm a success!

DANIEL

Are you?

GOODKIND

Huh?

DANIEL

Are you? What is success? Money? Yes; that's what our civilization tells us. Money! But where has that brought us? Only to the elevation of the unfit . . . the merely shrewd and predatory. All around us we see men of wealth who have nothing else . . . neither health nor happiness nor love nor respect. Men who can get no joy out of books, or pictures, or music, or even themselves. Tired, worried men who are afraid to quit because they have no resource except to make money—money with which to buy vulgar excitement for their own debased souls. Why, Mr. Goodkind, I have an income that you wouldn't suggest to your bookkeeper, but I have peace, and health, and friends, and time to read, and think, and dream, and help. Which of us is the rich man?

GOODKIND

But if everybody lived your way, what would become of the world's work?

DANIEL

Living that way is my contribution to the world's work. Another man's might be selling shoes, or writing plays, or digging ditches. Doing his job doesn't prevent any man from doing his bit. "From every man according to his ability, to every man according to his needs." And every man who gives his best must find his happiness.

GOODKIND

I'm afraid there wouldn't be much progress . . . living your way.

DANIEL

That's the second time you've spoken of my way. It isn't *my* way. It's the sum total of all that has been learned and taught. You, and Jerry, and the others have called me eccentric, and a fool, because I'm trying to walk a path trod hard by countless feet. Was Christ eccentric? Was Confucius a fool? And how about Buddha and Mohammed? What of St. Bernard, and St. Teresa, and St. Francis of Assisi—of Plato, and Zeno, and Lincoln, and Emerson, and Florence Nightingale, and Father Damien, and Octavia Hill, and all the saints and scientists, and poets and philosophers, who have lived and died in complete forgetfulness of self? Were they fools, or were they wise men and women who had found the way to peace and happiness? Were they failures, or were they the great successes of all Time and all Eternity?

GOODKIND

God knows!

[JERRY *enters . . . a dying man. He drags his legs
with difficulty, and his speech is thick, but he is
still cynical and defiant.*]

JERRY

Well, you've been the devil of a time! I came up to
see what was keeping you!

GOODKIND

[*Rising*]: Mr. Gilchrist.

JERRY

Hello, Gilchrist!

DANIEL

[*Crossing to C.*]: How are you, Jerry?

JERRY

Not so damned well! But I'll be all right in the
Spring! Clare's looking after me. Clare's a good
sport. What I need now's a run down to Palm Beach!
[*Looks around*] So you're reduced to this, are you?

DANIEL

Yes.

JERRY

Going to take my job?

DANIEL

No.

JERRY

Why not?

DANIEL

Your father understands.

JERRY

Yes . . . so do I! Didn't I always say you were a nut? That's it; a nut! [*He laughs with a laugh that begins to get the better of him.*]

GOODKIND

[*Crossing rapidly to the door*]: Come, Jerry!
[*A light rap; GOODKIND opens. Enter MARY MAR-GARET. She glances at him and crosses to upper L. C. JERRY looks at her, and turns back to DAN.*]

JERRY

Who's the girl?

DANIEL

Your father's waiting.

JERRY

A' right! . . . [*Crosses L.*] Some failure *you've* made out of life! [*Turns back and leers at MARY MARGARET. In the doorway, looks at DAN.*] Wheels . . . by God! Wheels! [*He laughs, and exits.*]

GOODKIND

[*Goes to DAN and takes his hand*]: I wonder if *you're* the failure, after all. [*Returns to the door.*] Good-night! [*He exits.*]
[*DAN takes his pipe from his pocket and puts it in his mouth. Some chimes, in the distance, begin the*

anthem "Hark the Herald Angels Sing." DANIEL goes up, draws back the curtains, and throws open the window. MARY MARGARET, feeling the fresh air, draws her furs about her, happily. She turns up. DANIEL is standing with his left arm akimbo. MARY MARGARET slips her head through it, and nestles to him. They . . . and we . . . see the chimney pots, and the blue night sky, and one bright star.]

MARY MARGARET

Mr. Gilchrist! Is that the Star of Bethlehem?

DANIEL

I wonder. [*The chimes swell out, and*

THE CURTAIN FALLS